John Parmiter came to faith
working for a property con
of a life spent living out tha
the values and commands
changing, and urgently nee
Nicky Gumbel, Vicar of Holy Trinity Brompton, London

Ten at Work shows us how to have a real faith in a real world . . . If
you are in the world of work, you need to read and think through
what is written here.
J.John (Canon), www.philotrust.com, from the Foreword

John Parmiter is a man full of honesty, integrity and practical,
biblical wisdom. As with the man, so with the book. *Ten at Work*
is packed full of precious pearls that help in the quest to live out
our faith at work.
*Jago Wynne, Curate at Holy Trinity Brompton, former Workplace
Minister at All Souls, Langham Place, and author of* Working
Without Wilting

TEN AT WORK

To David Prior: speaker, writer, prophet, sage,
sometime public preacher in the Diocese of London,
an original teacher to the marketplace

With much gratitude from a student

John Parmiter

TEN AT WORK

Living the commandments in your job

ivp

INTER-VARSITY PRESS
Norton Street, Nottingham NG7 3HR, England
Email: ivp@ivpbooks.com
Website: www.ivpbooks.com

First published 2011

British Library Cataloguing in Publication Data
A catalogue record for this book is available from the British Library.

ISBN: 978–1–84474–557–9

Set in Dante 12 / 15pt
Typeset in Great Britain by CRB Associates, Potterhanworth, Lincolnshire
Printed and bound in Great Britain by Ashford Colour Press Ltd, Gosport,
Hampshire

CONTENTS

SERIES PREFACE

A time for courage

Work matters hugely.

Work is the primary activity God created us to pursue – in communion with him and in partnership with others. Indeed, one of work's main goals is to make God's world a better place for all God's creatures to flourish in – to his glory.

Yes, work matters hugely.

And to many people it brings the joys of purpose shared, relationships deepened, talents honed, character shaped, obstacles overcome, products made, people served and money earned – even amid the inevitable frustrations, failures and disagreements of working life in even the best of organizations.

Yes, work matters hugely. And the financial crisis that began in 2008 only served to reinforce that reality as many found themselves without paid employment, many more with less money and many, many more were gripped by the fear of losing their jobs. However, long before the crisis, work had been getting harder, longer, less satisfying and more draining. Work had stretched its voracious tentacles into almost every area of life, sucking out the zing and whoosh and ease from time with family, friends, hobbies and community activities. UK citizens, for example, work four hours longer per person per week than the citizens of any other EU nation. We live in Slave New World.

How do we follow Jesus faithfully and fruitfully in such conditions?

Is coping – getting through the week – the height of our ambition? Surely not. But do we have good news for the workplace? Not just a truth to proclaim but a way to follow?

Not just a way to follow but life, divine life, to infuse the quality of our work, the quality of our relationships at work, and the quality of our contribution to the culture of the organizations in which we work? In our current context, we need not only biblical insight and divine empowerment, but also courage to make tough decisions about work and life, and courage to make tough decisions at work. Furthermore, at this time of national soul-searching about our economy and the values that drive it, we need to learn not only how to be faithful servants in the work culture we find ourselves in, but also to become proactive, positive shapers of that culture.

That's what the Faith at Work series is designed to do: take on the tough issues facing workers and offer material that's fresh, either because it brings new insights to familiar topics or because the author's particular background and experience open up enlightening vistas. We've also tried to write the books so that there's something nutritious and tasty, not only for the leisurely diner, but also for the snacker snatching a quick read on a train, or in a break, or, indeed, at the end of a demanding day.

The Lord be with you as you read. And the Lord be with you as you seek to follow him faithfully and courageously in your workplace.

Mark Greene, Series Editor
London Institute for Contemporary Christianity
2009

Volumes include:
Get a Life Paul Valler
Working It Out Ian Coffey
Working Without Wilting Jago Wynne
Working Models for Our Time Mark Greene (commissioned)

FOREWORD

I'm delighted to commend to you this book on applying the Ten Commandments at work, for four reasons:

This is a *profound* book. I can't imagine that many people have preached on the Ten Commandments as often as I have, yet I have found fresh insights on every page. Time and time again John Parmiter finds new (but always biblical) perspectives on these well-known words. There are years of thought distilled into these pages.

This is a *practical* book. This is no abstract theological study but a thought-provoking manual on how to do what's right in a world that wants you to do what's wrong. This book is full of relevant and useful insights into how to live out everything that the Ten Commandments stand for in the increasingly challenging world of business. This challenge to workplace witness is desperately needed. There are too many Christians whose faith seems to get left at home when they travel to work. At best that makes their faith irrelevant, at worst, hypocritical. *Ten at Work* shows us how to have a real faith in a real world.

This is a *provocative* book. Because this book is so firmly set in the everyday world of business, contracts and negotiations – a world that can often seem removed from our faith – it constantly challenges us to think about how we live our lives. If you are in the world of work, you need to read and think through what is written here. After all, if you are not a Christian in the office, in what sense are you a Christian?

Finally, it is a *prophetic* book. In case you hadn't noticed, the world of business and finance hasn't exactly been the model of high moral standards over the last few years. There is much in this book that tells us why and how business (big and small) can go rotten. Yet it also carries the message of hope that, if Christians could live out the principles of the Ten Commandments in the workplace, the world of commerce and business might be a very different place.

John Parmiter graciously acknowledges my own influence on his thinking. Let me return the compliment: I have learned from him. This book has been insightful, instructive and inspirational to me. May it also be the same to you.

J.John (Canon)
www.philotrust.com

INTRODUCTION

The commandments, 'Do not commit adultery,' 'Do not murder,'
'Do not steal,' 'Do not covet,' and whatever other commandment
there may be, are summed up in this one rule: 'Love your
neighbour as yourself.' Love does no harm to its neighbour.
Therefore love is the fulfilment of the law. And do this,
understanding the present time.
(Romans 13:9–11a)

Love

'Love makes one fit for any work' (George Herbert).[1]

Loving others can be quite a challenge, especially at work:
the foreman might be a bully, fellow teachers might be under-
mining, the commanding officer intimidating, the manager
a liar, or the ward sister a tyrant. On the other hand, your
boss may be an inspiration and your colleagues incredibly
supportive. For most of us our workplace is a pretty mixed
place in terms of positives and negatives, whether it's in the
store, hospital, library, office, warehouse, or whatever setting
you find yourself in. Even if you work from home you will
still face challenges from those with whom you interact or
do business.

It may seem surprising to apply love specifically to the
context of our work environment. But that is the amazing
message of the gospel – that God's love for us is just as relevant
there as in other spheres of life.

Love and relationships are essentially what the commandments are about. God gave them to us out of love: as

protection, to define our freedom (from guilt and shame) and as a framework for our relationships. The commandments sum up the central teaching of Jesus – love God, love your neighbour.

Jesus reminds his hearers of the centrality of the commandments to our love relationship with God: 'If you obey my commands, you will remain in my love' (John 15:10); and 'If you want to enter life, obey the commandments' (Matthew 19:17). They are not so concerned with our outward behaviours – though they must follow – as with what is going on in our hearts. So, for example, the tenth commandment ('Do not covet') is not just about the protection of someone else's property, but relates to the spiritual condition of the individual concerned. Indeed, all the commandments address the condition of the human heart.

Our response to God's love is twofold: to love God by living in obedience to his commands; and to demonstrate what that love looks like in our own lives and in loving others.

We demonstrate our love for God by following him in our hearts and by obeying his commands in our actions. One flows to the other. We are thankful for what he has done, and our lives show it, including at work.

The promise
These commands are not to be seen as heavy obligations that God has laid on people – as rules of some repressive religious regime – but as promises. Like Israel, we too can find the commandments burdensome and too often we fail to keep them. But God announced through the prophet Ezekiel: 'I will give you a new heart and put a new spirit in you; I will remove from you your heart of stone and give you a heart of flesh. And I will put my Spirit in you and move you to

follow my decrees and be careful to keep my laws' (Ezekiel 36:26–27).

This is God's work in us; this is how he makes his otherwise burdensome obligations into living promises. He is working this out in our working lives, as we submit our whole lives to the lordship of Jesus Christ.

Therefore the commandments are to be seen, through the lens of the cross, as promises: promises that the Spirit of God is enabling us to work out through these commands as the fruit of our lives, as God transforms our hearts. The Spirit of God 'moves us' (in the words of Ezekiel) to act differently: 'You shall not steal' becomes 'I will not steal.' I lose any desire or inclination to do so. As Paul writes to the Galatians, 'So I say, live by the Spirit, and you will not gratify the desires of the sinful nature . . . If you are led by the Spirit, you are not under law' (Galatians 5:16, 18). The work of God transforms what was a burdensome law into our heart's desire.

The work of Jesus on the cross and of his Holy Spirit in our lives also transforms our perspective. We now do not so much ask 'What would Jesus do?' as 'What is Jesus *doing*?' I now trust him to do in me what he wants; not to struggle and strive alone, which is how so many of us feel when we walk into work.

Good news

This is good news! It is such a relief to know that it's not all down to us; that we don't have to strain, like slaves under the command of an unforgiving overseer. We don't have to feel that work is something to be endured or survived, as so many do (including myself at times).

We can draw great comfort from the gospel because God has already taken the initiative to rescue us from slavery and reconcile us to himself and the world. He has taken the initiative to restore our relationship with him, through the work that his Son Jesus Christ has done on the cross. And he has sent his Holy Spirit to be our guide and counsellor.

Our work life, as part of our whole life, can now be lived in response to what Jesus has already done. He has won the victory on the cross, and we are now 'in Christ' (2 Corinthians 5:17) if we have put our trust in him. And God has not stopped taking the initiative with us.

'Understanding the present time'

'Most of our sinful desires can be fed by things in our culture' (Tim Chester).[2]

Scripture challenges us to work at understanding the culture of our workplaces: 'And do this, understanding the present time' (Romans 13:11a). It's not surprising that many of the problems we experience lie in the *culture* of our work. This can be sector-wide, such as how MPs claimed expenses, or local – like how teachers treat one another in the staffroom. For example, the atmosphere in your depot might be a critical one, infecting all who work there; or in the office the boss might shame staff in public, causing his subordinates down the line to do the same. On the other hand, your manager may be a positive encourager whose attitude influences his or her subordinates as well. These are behaviours, good and bad, that take root in a work culture and they can be contagious.

Anne Wilson Schaef and Diane Fassel write: 'If your life is taken up by lying to your self and others, attempting to control, perfectionism, denial, grabbing what you can for yourself, and refusing to let in information that would alter the addictive paradigm, then you are spiritually bankrupt.'[3] I believe that the solutions to many workplace issues are not going to be fixed by external regulators. The solutions are spiritual, and the place that needs fixing is the hearts of individuals: which means you and me.

I was struck by a letter written by a group of sixteen business leaders to the *Financial Times* in 2010 in the wake of the outcry about bank failures, corporate greed and collapses within the financial systems. These leaders wanted to 'create, oversee and imbue their organizations with an enlightened culture based on professionalism and integrity'. Why did they write? One commentator said it was because they believe the City has lost its moral compass and they realize it's up to them to lead the way, as something as basic as a culture of integrity cannot be imposed by a regulator from outside.

Where will those leaders, and others, find their solutions? We must go back to foundational principles, and nothing is as foundational as the Ten Commandments. As we do so, we will discover how relevant they are to our working lives.

Making the workplace better

Our work can dominate our whole life, and for many of us the workplace has also become the primary source of our social life. Work can be great, and for some of us it is a place of fulfilment, satisfaction and just reward. But for many of us it is a hard place, involving stress, long hours, conflict, managers we don't trust and real difficulties in achieving balance with the rest of our life. Work is becoming increasingly insecure and, as surveys tell us, less meaningful. The message of this book is that there *is* a way in which work life can be better, and one where we as individual Christians can make a difference.

Christian thinking about the workplace has become more urgent as we witness the see-saw effects of the marketplace, and the dominating culture of greed during the boom years has changed to one of fear, as the credit-crunch has developed into full-blown recession. Both greed and fear have deeply corrosive effects on the workplace, and neither the upward nor the downward cycles necessarily produce conditions conducive to a satisfying or meaningful work life. So we must address our work culture.

The underlying issues we face at work and in business are not new, though they will have new guises. It was Alan Greenspan, the former Chairman of the US Federal Reserve, who pointed out: 'It is not that humans have become any more greedy than in generations past. It is that the avenues to express greed have grown so enormously.'

These are not just 'someone else's' issues either. In every local situation there is a 'me' or a 'you' – a real person. Each of us will be called to account. We cannot escape responsibility for our own individual actions and our part in situations in which we find ourselves. We cannot simply hide behind the decisions of our union, head teacher, store manager or chief executive.

The health of our work culture is very significant, and when it gets sick it affects the whole of society. The turmoil in the financial markets, the banking crises, the greed of some corporations and the scandals of Parliament are all in large measure due to faults in our work culture. And that culture is becoming increasingly morally bankrupt, value-free and corrosively dehumanizing. In the boom times, the London Institute for Contemporary Christianity (LICC) made this comment in one of its weekly emails:

> It's not surprising that managers are craving meaning from
> their jobs when, according to other research, they have
> precious little time for anything else. Nor is it surprising that
> they aren't finding it because, despite the rhetoric of corporate

values statements, today's workplace is in reality almost
entirely focused on a line – profit . . . Indeed, one of the
greatest challenges facing Christians in the UK is to live the
abundant life of Christ in the face of the dehumanizing,
relationally destructive and emotionally, physically and
spiritually debilitating effects of the contemporary work-place.[4]

So all is not well in the workplace. There is a continuing
breakdown of trust at all levels and loss of confidence in the
management of our schools, public services, corporations,
the professions and those who regulate them. I meet people
who are increasingly enslaved by their work; some are even
addicted to it. Insecurity is an all-too-common experience.
Arrogance is endemic in some quarters, while bullying is a
significant growing problem. Stress levels are high – so high
in places that some can only get through the day on a line of
charlie. And relationships are often poor and painful.

Solutions needed

The pundits wonder where we are to find solutions. They
realize that solutions are not to be found just in economics
or the application of ethics, important as they are, and they
are absolutely right. Nor is it simply an issue of complying
with external regulations. No, the regulators will not save us.
There is a deeper, spiritual malaise that needs to be addressed.

But as Christians we have good news to proclaim, a new
life to live out and God's ways to share. Perhaps we have been
too quiet for too long. It was good to hear the Roman Catholic
Archbishop of Westminster say in a recent Christmas address:

Christians neither condemn nor canonize the market
economy; it may be an essential element in the conduct of
human affairs. But we have to remember that it is a system

governed by people, not some blind force like gravity. Those
who operate the market economy have an obligation to act
in ways that promote the common good . . . the market
economy will only work justly if it has an underlying moral
purpose.[5]

As Christians, we have much to contribute by explaining that
purpose. Our task is essentially to say and do the right thing
on a daily basis. For when we say or do even the smallest
thing, we open up a door to heaven and we just don't know
what God will do when he comes in.

Yet I fear that many Christians are too isolated, too pres-
surized or just feel paralysed. So many lack confidence or do
not believe they can make a difference. And that 'difference'
is not usually some heroic act of whistle-blowing or a stand
for the gospel. It is more likely to be some small deed or word
in a local situation, such as not passing on gossip in the
changing room, speaking up for a vulnerable but unpopular
pupil in the staffroom, or befriending an upset co-worker at
the water cooler.

In this book I want to demonstrate how the Ten Commandments can liberate us to work well, how we can be at
peace about being a Christian at work and how we can grow
in confidence in order to be those who make a difference.

But where do we start? The beginning is a good place, and
nothing is as foundational to God's directions to us as the Ten
Commandments, given out of his love for his people, to
govern their covenant relationship with him: 'I will be your
God; you will be my people' (see Exodus 6:7). The first four
commandments concern our relationship with God; the
remaining six refer to our relationships with one another and,
in the context of God's special relationship with Israel, the
wider world.

So central are the Ten Commandments to the covenant God made with his people that when Solomon had the ark finally brought into the temple, it contained only the tablets that had been given to Moses.

Alternatives?

There is a prevailing view that the Ten Commandments are no longer relevant. For example, a few years ago Channel 4 staged a two-hour Saturday prime-time blockbuster, *The New Ten Commandments*, with Jon Snow in the role of Moses. But instead of hearing from God, he consulted a massive, two-part poll involving over 44,000 people from across the UK. Ordinary people were heard to remark: 'If we can't remember them can they be relevant?' or 'I don't think we need them any more.' Jon Snow reflected what many were feeling when he quoted survey responses such as: 'They spoil our enjoyment' and 'They are a flawed product.'

The participants were invited to redraw the commandments. In the popular revised list, now a top twenty, four of God's originals had made a quick exit. The commandments to have no other gods and not to commit adultery were retained in the lower rankings of the top twenty, and a new version of the fifth commandment ('Respect your parents') survived at number eleven. 'Do not murder' and 'Do not steal' even made it into the top five. The majority of the new commandments voiced genuine, strongly felt popular sentiments: try your best; enjoy life; protect your family; look after the vulnerable; protect the environment; be honest; and take responsibility for your actions (appearing at number two).

The programme's research came up with a top 'new' commandment, which was head and shoulders above the rest. By a landslide vote, and receiving four times more votes than its nearest rival, was: 'Treat others as you would have them treat you.' But is this so new? Jesus ended one of his discourses with these words: 'In everything, do to others what you would have them do to you, for this sums up the Law and the Prophets' (Matthew 7:12).

One of the main reasons why there has been renewed interest in the Ten Commandments, as with this programme, is that deep within us we know that something is going wrong in our world. In our workplaces we *know* that things are far from what they should be. We sense we are off-track and that we desperately need to get back on it. But not all of us know what that track is.

There *is* a better way to live and work. I believe passionately that we need to recover the foundational value of the Ten Commandments – for each of us individually, as well as corporately for our workplaces and for the way in which business is conducted. I believe that we are all searching for an authentic life. That means one life – not two lives: worklife/homelife, or public/private, the Sunday me/Monday me. It means authentic, real, thoroughly integrated, genuine life – not some living death or a working life that we manage to survive on a week-by-week (or even day-by-day) basis. We want a full, balanced, working life with healthy relationships.

What must we do?

At one level the answer is that there is actually nothing to *do*. When the people were fed on the mountainside and later indicated they wanted to respond to Jesus' message, they asked him: 'What must we do to do the works God requires?' Jesus simply answered, 'The work of God is this: to believe in the one he has sent' (John 6:28, 29).

To do works for God risks slipping into legalism, as there is nothing we can actually do to earn his approval. As Jesus pointed out later in his ministry, the Christian life is impossible without God (Mark 10:27). First and foremost the Christian life is to believe in Jesus. What he offers us is pure grace, undeserved and at a great price to himself.

But of course, at another level we do want to do the right thing – not good works, but righteous action, out of love. So in the final chapter we want to explore some of the ways in which we can work out our faith in a loving God by loving actions in our places of work and thereby push back the unrighteousness we find in the workplace.

A journey

I attended a faith-based school which put me off religion and left me with no real beliefs at all. I embarked on what became a reasonably successful career, got married and started to have children. I had no real issues in my life at that time; I just wanted to get on.

However, my wife came to faith after we had been married about seven years, when three of our four children had been born, and that started the questions. When we had our children baptized I just couldn't say the words on the card; I felt like a hypocrite. But it was when our second child was diagnosed with leukaemia at the age of three that things came to a head. My wife, who had been a Christian only six months, taught him to pray. He would then ask me to pray for 'God's healing power'! And when I did, I witnessed healings that I couldn't make sense of for some time. (Simon is now grown up and happily married, as are all our four children. Today, he is a teacher with a little boy of his own.) So two years later, after hearing one of David Watson's last evangelistic talks, I came to faith. I was thirty-three at the time and an ambitious young associate in a large property advisory firm in London.

I had to make sense of what my new faith meant in a successful business environment. What did it now mean to be ambitious? How was I to negotiate? I had lots of questions that needed answering. I learned little from church, but I attended Midweek in Mayfair, a Christian marketplace ministry in London's West End, and with the help of Revd David Prior and others I found the means to relate my faith in Jesus to a pressured world that largely ignored him. I subsequently became a trustee, speaker, mentor and coach with Midweek. I have tried to bring to this book what I have learned and studied over the last twenty-five years while leading and growing my professional practice.

Writing this book has been both exciting and daunting: exciting, to set down what I have learned in a book (so publicly), but also daunting, as I have failed to live up to the standard so many times. How can I, as one who falls so often, have the gall to write about these things to so many who shine like stars in their own workplace? I have put the writing of this book aside too often by listening to that one. It has also been a challenging couple of years as I have battled through the recession. But I have been sufficiently encouraged to soldier on by others who, despite knowing my failures, think there is something worthwhile to say on this subject.

I have worked in central London all my life, mainly in the property-based sector, specializing in planning consultancy. I have been a local government officer, a junior professional, an equity partner, a company director and self-employed. These experiences have obviously affected my perspective and the examples I use. I hope, nevertheless, that I have been able to make this book applicable to you, whatever your line or mode of work, whether in the public sector, in a large organization, as part of a small business or working for yourself.

What I have found overall is that at work, as in life, true freedom is not found 'out there', but 'in here' – in our hearts – and within the secure boundaries designed by our Creator God who loves us: a framework we know as the Ten Commandments.

Ten

I start this book with the tenth commandment, following the model set by J.John. As I sat in an enormous tent on Clapham Common one summer's day, I was riveted by his presentation of the commandments and the relevance of his 'how-to' themes. The response among the audience was humbling to watch. Could such themes be applied more directly to the workplace, I wondered? I went to see him later and he was good enough to give me his time, his blessing and much encouragement to develop this material for the workplace.

Together we sketched out the format of what were at first a series of talks given in the City during 2005 and, later as the material developed, at LICC in 2009 and 2011. I am deeply grateful for all J.John's encouragement and for the opportunity to draw on the structure and content of his book – *Ten*. But any disappointments with the material in this book are entirely down to me.

I am following J.John's lead in starting with the tenth commandment and ending with the first. The first commandment is the core, the radiant central truth. We will approach it gently and not rush. We will start at the edge and work our way towards it.

The Ten Commandants were not given as topics for discussion; but as tools to freedom, to be lived out in obedience. Come with me, if you will, to discover over the next ten chapters a new freedom, a new authentic life and the confidence to make a difference in your workplace, as we uncover the power of these truths and find liberation in living them out at work.

1. DISCOVERING CONTENTMENT

*You shall not covet your neighbour's house. You shall not covet
your neighbour's wife, or his manservant or maidservant,
his ox or donkey, or anything that belongs to your neighbour.*
(Exodus 20:17)

Your promotion was great until you heard who else had been promoted; you were happy with your new wages until you heard about your colleague's rise; you were satisfied with the new equipment until the other team got even better kit; or you were pleased with your team's sales results until the competition produced theirs. We can all add similar examples of our own. Often we allow our thoughts to rob us of the ability to be content with what we have.

We need to avoid that gnawing thought process that starts with 'if only . . . ': if only I had the equipment *they* have I could do my job properly; if only we had *that* competitor leading us we would do all right; if only we had a *different* head teacher we could be a better school.

'Covet' is not a common word these days: it means to desire something that is not ours. The Hebrew word implies more than just wanting something; it means actively to seek, yearn for, lust after or to acquire with evil intent. Commentators point out that the breaking of this commandment can be the gateway to violating every other principle in the Decalogue. John Durham therefore describes it as a 'summary commandment'.[1]

At the heart of this commandment is an attitude rather than a deed. This is certainly how Jesus approaches it in the Sermon on the Mount. He asserts that he has come to fulfil the Law and the Prophets, and in his teaching on murder and adultery he explains that the violation takes place in our hearts (Matthew 5:21–30).

The work context

The language used in this commandment is strikingly practical. But how does it translate into modern workplace terminology?

First, our neighbour is anyone else! In the well-known parable of the Good Samaritan Jesus explains that our neighbour is *all* other people, more than just the people who work alongside us. In our workplace or work contexts it could be our competitors, a rival team in our organization, or simply our colleagues.

Secondly, this commandment refers to six areas of life that are highly relevant to the world of work:

- A **house** is an important asset, but so is a factory, a warehouse, a retail store, a school, a hospital or any real estate, or a portfolio of another organization's assets.
- A **wife** (and this includes a husband, of course) refers to right relationships: with customers, colleagues, staff, competitors, suppliers, clients and so on.
- A **manservant** includes employees, contractors, freelancers, temporary staff and even competitors' staff or a rival team. It also relates to the controversial area of poaching staff.
- An **ox** was the beast of burden, the necessary means of production. In today's terms this could be the plant and machinery, tools and equipment, intellectual property, software and business systems.
- A **donkey** was the means of transport. For us today that would include distribution systems, pipelines,

warehouses, air transport, shipping and the whole world of logistics.
- **Anything** – is anything! Anything that belongs to someone else, that is theirs and not yours or mine.

Coveting concerns all these things. It is an activity, a process or a way of thinking that will *harm* us. That is why God has prohibited it. It is not the vindictive edict of some grumpy old man in the sky, but of a loving Creator who knows us so well. He knows what we are like, what we are capable of and where we are vulnerable.

The apostle John knew the lure of the world:

> Do not love the world . . . For everything in the world – the cravings of sinful man, the lust of his eyes and the boasting of what he has and does – comes not from the Father but from the world. The world and its desires pass away, but the man who does the will of God lives for ever.
> (1 John 2:15–17)

Relativities

Coveting starts very early on in life: put two small children in a room and give them just one toy between them, and then stand back and observe how long it takes for one of them to grab that toy and say, 'Mine!'

We are preoccupied by relativities. For some years I was a partner in a large West End property firm. I got to see what all the partners were earning. Every year the senior partner called us into his office to discuss rewards – our own *and* to hear our views on our partners'. What fascinated me was the fact that virtually without exception my partners, although concerned about their own pay, were also deeply keen to ensure that they were being paid *no less* than their peers.

'Think not so much of what you have not, as of what you have' (Marcus Aurelius).

Despite all the recent growth in economic wealth, British and US surveys reveal the shocking fact that we are actually no happier than we were fifty years ago. Money alone does not lead to increased happiness once a basic and very low threshold is met (some say as little as £20,000 a year). Why is this? Because we are comparing our incomes with those of other people. But in a richer society the Joneses are getting richer too! So the attempt at relative betterment always fails; it never satisfies.

Our desires, of course, are being moulded by the world around us. Advertising really works, because advertising fuels a basic human desire for more. It feeds off the Great Lie that somehow 'one more' or 'a bit more' will satisfy. I despaired once when, after I had given a talk on a similar subject, a highly respectable Christian surveyor came up to me and said, 'I know . . . but an extra twenty grand would solve so much . . .'

Another approach?

In Channel 4's *The New Ten Commandments*, this particular commandment was trashed; it didn't even make it into the new top twenty. Jon Snow commented that the media have changed standards for everyone. 'Where would we be?' people asked. 'Advertising's asking us to covet!' they explained.

In the programme, people around the UK took part in various exercises to ascertain how far they would go in order to obtain something they really wanted. In one test a brand-new, top-of-the-range Lamborghini was on offer. What would three members of the public be prepared to do to get it? Well, one man would cut off his left leg, another was willing to sell his soul, and yet another was even prepared to give up one of his children! I watched this with mouth wide open.

But the conclusion wasn't quite as dire as that exercise implied. The new popular top twenty included two additions: 'Appreciate what you have' (number twelve) and 'Live within your means' (number sixteen). 'It's important to be content,' participants said.

Thoughts and actions

While we may not turn all our desires into actions, all our actions are the result of our desires: every theft originates with a thought; every land grab starts with a desire; every act of adultery begins in the mind. The thought may not break the law, but its consequences may quickly lead in that direction. It may be impossible to legislate against the thought, but its effects are seen everywhere, and they can be devastating.

We do not need to look very far to see the negative consequences. In the world of work we see people getting hurt – perhaps due to the following:

- pension schemes that have been raided, plunging thousands into difficulty in their retirement;
- asset-stripping that leaves factories empty and former employees forced to be idle and jobless;
- a loan that is called in aggressively, pushing a company into bankruptcy and its employees out of work;
- cost-cutting programmes in public services – some of which may be motivated by political slogans or one-upmanship – leading to redundancies and a climate of fear among staff;
- takeovers motivated by empire building, leaving managements and staff out of work;

- boosting cash-flow by late payment, causing hardship for suppliers and contractors.

Other examples could be added to the list.

What about poaching?

A financial services firm hit the headlines with its move to lure up to eighty highly paid staff from two rival firms, who then accused them of launching a 'legally questionable, early Spring, poaching offensive'.[2] The legalities centred on the restrictions imposed on the people concerned. The newspaper article focused on the mayhem in financial centres around the world caused by such big money moves, as clearly the endless process of poaching (now we win, now we lose) has its own costs. But the more serious question was never asked: is it moral?

I have asked this myself, as one who has sought to attract new people to my firm. Does this kind of activity breach the tenth commandment?

Motivations

Covetousness is motivated by greed and fear: the same two great dynamics that have so dramatically affected the recent turmoil of the world's markets. These twin motivations underpin so much of the activity we see in force in the workplace.

Greed

When John D. Rockefeller was the richest man in the world, he was asked: 'How much money does it take for a person to be really satisfied?' He answered, 'Just a little bit more'. His reply was revealing of the human condition: we just yearn for a bit more.

God is deeply concerned to protect us from our base motives. Jesus warned the crowd: 'Watch out! Be on your guard against all kinds of greed; a man's life does not consist in the abundance of his possessions' (Luke 12:15).

The Bible does not condemn money or wealth, but it is very realistic about it: 'For the *love* of money is a root of all *kinds* of evil' (1 Timothy 6:10, emphasis added). This verse is often misquoted. God is not opposed to money, but he is opposed to the *worship* of it. Too many people in work do worship it. It is a bad master but a good servant. At money's altar we sacrifice our contentment, for it will *never* satisfy.

But it's not just more money that we yearn for. We can long for more power: even in our own small team someone always wants to be in charge. So we plot and scheme and edge others out of the way . . . We want a greater reputation and more status, so we actively seek after them. Many want to be better than the next person. For example, they want to be seen as:

- the hardest on the shop floor
- the most aggressive in the team
- topping the sales targets month after month
- doing the most deals
- the favourite
- playing the hardest
- the most important
- whatever . . . it doesn't always matter what it is!

Power and paperclips

When I worked in local government, the man who ran the council's stationery department was actually quite powerful in his own small sphere. He ran his modest department in a way that had everyone quaking in their boots when they wanted to place an order. The joke was that if you requested two paperclips he would ask who the other one was for! He was a tough, burly Scot who often wore his kilt (all part of the drama he created) and so became known as Bill McKnees. No-one would dare to cross him.

On another occasion I was asked to reorganize a department in the firm. It soon became apparent that the established manager's secretary was the real power on that floor: she was the one I had to win over, not just her boss.

Fear

Fear is a major driver of the marketplace and also of covetousness. We worry about not having enough; we also worry about losing what we have, as the more we earn, the more commitments we enter into: a larger house with a larger mortgage, more holidays and more appearances to keep up.

And so fear of losing our job becomes ever more significant and will eventually grip us. We take what is not ours to shore up our position. We divert equipment or resources in our direction; we intercept orders meant for others; we may even start to take the credit for things we didn't do. It can be very destructive very quickly. But unless we are prepared to trust God with our job, we will ultimately be a slave to it, relying on our own strategies and devices to maintain what security it offers.

Jesus says, 'Therefore I tell you, do not worry about your life, what you will eat or drink; or about your body, what you will wear. Is not life more important than food, and the body more important than clothes?' He goes on to explain and concludes: 'But seek first [God's] kingdom and his righteousness, and all these things will be given to you as well. Therefore do not worry about tomorrow, for tomorrow will worry about itself. Each day has enough trouble of its own' (Matthew 6:25, 33–34).

We need to be aware of the *power* of covetousness. It can get a grip on our lives. But when we name it, we can face it. Tell God; tell someone you trust (perhaps someone you are accountable to); tell your vicar or pastor what is an issue for you and bring it out into the light.

What we are aiming for is what Paul says to Timothy: 'But godliness with contentment is great gain' (1 Timothy 6:6).

Cooperating with God

So how might we cooperate with what God is doing in our lives and rediscover contentment in our work? How might we see a reduction of covetousness in our lives? And how might we sow contentment around us? I suggest six ways in which we can cooperate with the work of the indwelling Spirit of Jesus in our lives:

1. Cultivate our knowledge of the Creator

So often it is the world around us that shapes our behaviour and thinking. For many of us the most significant influence is our work environment or the dominant workplace culture. But Romans 12:2 helps us here: 'Don't let the world around you squeeze you into its own mould' (J. B. Phillips).

The key to lasting contentment is to let God shape us, not our context. Contrary to popular opinion, he is not in the business of taking away our enjoyment and making us miserable. In Jeremiah 29:11 we read: '"For I know the plans I have for you," declares the LORD, "plans to prosper you and not to harm you, plans to give you hope and a future."'

We are in poor shape, however, to discover these plans, because of the condition of our hearts. Now this is the business God is in. A heart transplant is what happens when we come to know God through Jesus Christ, when we establish and maintain a relationship with God through his Son. He takes our self-absorbed, dysfunctional heart and replaces it with a new one, as he promised in Ezekiel: a heart that is moved to do things differently (Ezekiel 36:26–27).

2. Cultivate an attitude of gratitude

Covetousness robs us of what we *already* have. If in my heart I desire another woman at work, it will rob me of the appreciation I have for the wife I already have. If I desire a rival team, it will rob me of appreciation for the staff that I have. If I hanker for another's job, it will rob me of what satisfaction I already have. And so on. That is because the devil is a thief: he robs us.

So the best way to start the day is by thanking God. There's always something to thank him for: your job (if you have one), a beautiful day, being alive!, your home, your wife or husband, the beauty of creation, say on your way to work (I travel to my job by boat up the Thames and it is an amazing way to start my daily prayer time).

Another way is to thank others: the receptionist who greets you (mine doesn't, so each day is a battle to get eye contact when I say good morning), a subordinate for a job well done, a colleague for information provided and for small things done. It all makes such a difference: to you and to them.

3. Cultivate stewardship

At a funeral a relative was asked: 'Did Henry leave much?' To which came the reply: 'Yes, he left everything!'

True contentment is not found in having everything you want, but in not wanting to have everything. We come into the world with nothing and we take nothing out. Death strips us of all our possessions. What we have is, as it were, on loan and we are just stewards. I like the farmer's motto: 'Live as if you will die tomorrow; farm as if you will live for ever.'

In 1 Corinthians 3:21 Paul declares, 'All things are yours . . .' and he explains that true contentment is found not by holding out for more, but by holding what we have lightly.

We are temporary holders of our post or job (even if we work for ourselves). We are stewards of what we are given to do and of what we are enabled to do – whether we are stacking shelves or selling equipment, raising finance or teaching students. It will pass. We are only stewards.

Money, wealth and possessions do not buy us security. The world is so insecure that we pile up stuff now in order to feel more secure about the future. But as believers in Jesus Christ, we should be so sure about the future that we are able to live more securely in the present.

4. Cultivate relationships

We are to *love* people and *use* things. If we start to love things – status, targets, influence and so forth – we will end up using people. In our workplace we can be so stretched to get things done, that the individuals suffer.

The antidote to the danger of becoming too preoccupied with material possessions, money, wealth, status, when *things* become more important than *people*, is actively to cultivate relationships, both at home and at work.

Imagine this scenario: I wanted a better intern. My colleague has one and is getting a lot of support on her projects. I try to get hers to do as much work for me as possible, but that puts a strain on my relationship with my colleague. I am frustrated with my intern so I get short with him when he doesn't understand; I become even more irritated with him when he gets things wrong. And then I begin to see what the problem is – it's me, not him. So I start to put in place measures that will help him to grow, and not find himself unsupported or in the firing line.

5. Cultivate giving

There is no greater antidote to the lure of money and possessions than giving. This is true in our home life as well as at work. We will be surprised by the freedom that comes from sharing resources rather than grasping them, and from sharing our time rather than guarding it jealously. We will want to covet less and give more.

A young missionary called Jim Elliot wrote: 'He is no fool who gives what he cannot keep, to gain what he cannot lose.' He wrote that at the age of twenty-two, and his life was taken seven years later. A similar exchange is true of money and possessions. We think that by coveting we will get them and by holding on to them we will keep them. But no, it is in the letting go that we can possess them, without them possessing us.

Jesus spoke a great deal about money and possessions – in sixteen out of his thirty-eight stories (or parables). He also said, 'It is more blessed to give than to receive' (Acts 20:35). As C. S. Lewis put it: 'Biblical charity is more than merely giving away that which we can afford to do without anyway. It is sacrificial in some way; it is about not expecting any return.'

So let us *give*. Giving can release the grip of possessions over us, and that will help to free us from coveting what is not ours.

6. Cultivate priorities

If we don't live by priorities, we will live by pressures. We can identify our priorities by examining our diaries and bank statements. How do we spend our time and money?

Jesus said,

> So do not worry, saying: 'What shall we eat?' or 'What shall
> we drink?' or 'What shall we wear?' For the pagans run after
> all these things, and your heavenly Father knows that you
> need them. But seek first his kingdom and his righteousness,
> and all these things will be given to you as well.
> (Matthew 6:31–33)

One of the most common complaints at work is: 'If only I
had more time . . . ' So many of us rob our home life in order
to make up the time we need at work, to earn extra wages,
to gain promotion, to finish a project, to win the manager's
approval (as she works so late). But priorities need prioritizing.
From a biblical perspective our priorities might be
expressed as: (1) God, (2) spouse, (3) family, (4) work, and
(5) church.

One of the most common mistakes is to confuse work
and family. We think that we can sacrifice our family in order
to gain at work, and we argue that our family will ultimately
gain from this. The other mistake is to confuse church and
God, and so we put church activities so high up our list of
priorities and thereby we sacrifice our work.

Yield to God

The workplace is challenging and we can make it more so by
desiring things we do not need, or worse, cannot have. This
spoils our relationship with God, it is detrimental to our relationships
with others, and it reduces our effectiveness as
change agents and witnesses to God where we work.

We can address this not so much by 'trying' as by 'yielding'
– to God. We need to allow him to work out his promises in
us and we must avoid getting in the way. We cultivate this

relationship with Jesus Christ through an active contentment in our workplace. He is the one who bears fruit in us – fruit that is good, fruit that will last.

For reflection

1. How content are you with your work situation?
2. How might you tackle any areas that you think of in terms of 'if only . . . '?
3. Do you compare yourself with other people? Why?
4. Do you need to repent of some of your own thought patterns?
5. Which of the suggested habits might you adopt?

2. REMAINING HONEST

You shall not give false testimony against your neighbour.
(Exodus 20:16)

Lies can have devastating effects in the workplace. A manager can block someone's promotion by giving a wrong impression about their performance. A shop-floor worker can put out a false rumour and so trash a co-worker's reputation. A prison officer's misleading report on an inmate can result in their incarceration for longer. A teacher's false assessment of a student can affect how the other teachers treat that person and may even blight his or her future.

Some people think that lies are mostly harmless or are only a temporary problem. Perhaps we talk about 'white lies'. But as we tell that 'little' lie to shift the blame off us, we transfer it on to someone else. We may have managed to get ourselves off the hook, but we have just put someone else on it. We adjust our timesheets to make ourselves look better, but we make someone else look worse. Someone always pays the bill for this kind of creativity. Lies have price tags.

Lies can start small. In a work situation I'm sure we have all experienced that feeling of being fobbed off with statements such as: 'Give me your number and I'll call you back'; 'We'll keep your application on file'; 'This will take two minutes to explain': or 'Let's have lunch some time.' Or have you ever found *yourself* making excuses, such as: 'I just didn't have time to finish it'; 'I didn't realize what was required'; 'She didn't make herself clear'; or, as is often the case, 'It wasn't my fault.'

Harmless or devastating?

False testimony matters to God. Proverbs 12:22 says, 'The LORD detests lying lips, but he delights in men who are truthful.'

Although the focus of the ninth command is 'our neighbour', its scope is far wider. Telling lies offends God, hurts us and undermines everyone's trust. It is not just a moral or ethical issue, it is also a spiritual matter. God is telling us that lies cause hurt and damage. God, in his love, has given us this command for our protection – for us personally and for the protection of others. The commandment is also given to reinforce our very integrity, which is important to God, as his people are to be his witnesses to the whole world.

In the Sermon on the Mount, Jesus teaches about oaths and concludes: 'Simply let your "Yes" be "Yes", and your "No", "No"; anything beyond this comes from the evil one' (Matthew 5:37). As ever, Jesus points at the activity of our hearts rather than our mouths.

The problem of trust

There is a growing lack of trust in corporate life, accelerated by the endemic use of spin and what LICC has called 'the mentality of the marketplace – find out what people want and then promise it to them'. In business there is a huge loss of confidence in our markets, with the collapse of banks, major government bailouts and the MPs' expenses scandal.

Increasingly we no longer believe what people say to us, especially our management. We are not even sure we believe what we read: in a HR circular; in the company mission statement; in a prospectus; in an analyst's report; in a CV or in a business plan. We have become cynical and there is a serious lack of trust.

In a past edition of *Management Today*, Richard Reeves, the Director of the Capital Eye Intelligence Agency, quoted a MORI poll, which found that only one person in ten thinks that company directors can be trusted to tell the truth. He commented that 'trustworthy people are not just hired, they are made'.[1]

This kind of problem in our work culture has been explored by Diane Fassel in her book *Working Ourselves to Death*.[2] She observes that problems with self-esteem can lead to a high degree of dishonesty, as people exaggerate their achievements and rarely mention their failures in the belief that people will not accept them for what they are.

One of the most frustrating people who ever worked for me was never wrong! Whatever the problem, it always seemed to be someone else's fault (or mine!). I survived her working for me for a year, and during that time she never ever admitted any failure, even when a client pointed it out directly.

Words

We have a truth decay problem which is exemplified by the wide range of euphemisms in common use in business:

- Statistics are 'massaged'
- Data are 'adjusted'
- Expenses are 'inflated'
- Financial reporting is 'inaccurate'
- Assets are 'misappropriated'
- Product defects are 'overlooked'
- Excuses are 'manufactured'
- Targets or deadlines 'slide'
- Pensions are 'mis-sold'
- Petrol stocks are 'overstated'
- Difficult issues are 'evaded'

- Mergers and acquisitions are 'over-promoted'
- Funds have suffered 'a temporary shortfall'

Far too often we resort to lying, and we see it all around us. What form it takes will depend on the context. For example, people in professional firms can lie about their billable hours. Is it really true what we hear the manager saying about others? Do we tell the whole truth when we negotiate? Companies lie to shareholders (perhaps about the extent of risks or accounting practices). Applicants lie to potential employers in their CVs (about the extent of real experience). People lie to the tax authorities in their returns. Companies lie to their lenders about their real capacity to repay.

Words and actions

In Matthew 21:28–32 Jesus tells a parable about a vineyard owner who had two sons, in order to teach the difference between words and actions (or the action of the heart). One son said he would work in the vineyard but later changed his mind and didn't do so. The other son refused to work but then did the work anyway. Only one obeyed the father. The bolshie employee is not always the problem.

Bernie Ebbers, the former CEO of WorldCom, was charged with multiple counts of fraud and conspiracy surrounding the $11 billion collapse of WorldCom in 2002. The prosecution alleged that Mr Ebbers had secretly instructed subordinates to cook the books to meet profit forecasts. Mr Ebbers claimed that he 'only looked after sales and marketing and the cost-reduction side of the business and knew nothing about complex accounting and finance'. The jury didn't believe him.

In my own work I negotiate planning permissions for new developments, and there can be a lot at stake. Sometimes I need to get objectors or politicians on side, and very occasionally I am told: 'John, tell them such and such . . . ' It is a rare occurrence, but when it happens I typically reply, 'But it's not true.' Sometimes I receive strange looks, as if to ask why that matters.

Telling the truth can be costly. In interview surveys of whistle-blowers in the US and UK, it was found that 80% of those who reported a fraud to which they were *not* a party ended up losing their jobs.

Reputation management

The furore over celebrity super-injunctions has opened up a new world of professional lying to more public scrutiny. It was found that celebrities were paying agencies to 'bury' bad news (or boost their rankings on search engines and review websites). This could cost them between £10,000 and £40,000 a month. As the founder of one agency said, 'You can't stop an event happening, but you can stop it being seen.' The agencies do this by hiring professional writers to draft suitable content which is posted on websites – typically using thousands of social networking profiles and employing false names to simulate the behaviour of real people, and so drive the real (often negative) stories down the list. Apparently most people don't read beyond the first page. A proud agency owner was quoted about one particular damage-limitation assignment in these terms: 'Within a week there were no longer any links to critical stories on the first page of results.'[3]

These 'reputation management' agencies are also used by authors, hotels, holiday organizers and others who want to see their products boosted by rave reviews on well-used websites and so improve sales or enhance their reputation, sometimes discrediting their rivals in the process. Teams of writers are required to write lies about them or their rivals.

The reputable search engines and websites try to root out the fraudsters, but as one agency was quoted as saying: 'You would use content writers who can switch between styles and vocabulary quite easily.' This is a corrosive practice and it is difficult to uncover.

Workplace scenarios

a. Gossip
Gossip is one of the most damaging activities at work. We love to gossip about the people we work with, work for or compete against. In fact anyone. The American journalist and gossip columnist Earl Wilson once said, 'Gossip is when you hear something you like about someone you don't.' Gossip is about repeating or passing on selective information about someone who is not there to defend themselves. When we hear someone being spoken about, it may turn out that they are neither part of the real problem, nor even part of the solution.

These gossipy conversations often take place when we come together as a group: in the canteen, the staff room, the changing room, the mess room, or when we pause at the copier, printer or water cooler. There is a moment when we can choose whether or not to join in, and the peer pressure can be quite intense. We need to know in advance what our response will be, as trying to work it out in the heat of the moment doesn't work.

b. Character assassination
This is a similar problem, but it is more direct. When someone is out of the room, or in a conversation with a client or a manager, we can say something that damages or even shatters that person's reputation and how he or she is seen by others. We can do people great harm in this way and perhaps leave

a trail of damage that the victim may never truly be able to put right. Reputations are hard earned but easily lost, and our reputations are vital to our careers, our effectiveness in the marketplace, and to our true identity.

Proverbs 26:20 says, 'Without wood a fire goes out; without gossip a quarrel dies down.'

We can often take part in this type of lying at work by hearing something about someone and replying with that deadly word: 'Yes . . . ', and trying to doubt it but without actually rebutting it or disengaging from it. This may do no more than sow doubt about the person, but it is a form of false testimony and can be harmful.

My son's experience is most unusual. He worked for a small Christian charity for three years. He summed up his experience of working there like this: 'It's a place where, when you leave the room, they say even *nicer* things about you than when you were there!'

c. Office politics

A recent survey found that 26% of the working population believe they fritter too much time on office politics and 15% of professionals spend upwards of three hours a week engaged in office politics. In another survey nearly half of CEOs, directors and senior managers cited office politics as their biggest bugbear. Not all this involves any form of false testimony, but enough does for it to be a problem.

I came across an alarming book entitled *The Way of the Rat: A Survival Guide to Office Politics*,[4] which has sold 70,000 copies in the author's native Netherlands. These are his top nine rules:

1. Always be on your guard and trust no-one.
2. Be a proactive rat and throw loyalty out of the window.

3. Learn how to undermine the boss.
4. Have no sympathy for people who claim to be victims at work.
5. Choose carefully who to suck up to.
6. If a project goes wrong, always blame one of your colleagues.
7. Choose the right moment to slag off your rivals.
8. Learn to tell 'truthful lies'.
9. Use as many words as you can to say as little as possible about what you are up to.

If this book is selling even half the number of copies reported, I think we have a problem.

d. Negotiation

When I was more involved with Christians in Property (a contradiction in terms, one person once told me!), we did a training event for young Christian surveyors. We started by identifying the work-related issues they faced. The number-one issue by a long way was: how can I negotiate with integrity (in other words without lying)?

How does your union negotiate? Or your estate agent when you buy a house, or your lawyer when you are entering into an agreement? We also have a responsibility to ensure that those acting on our behalf are doing so with integrity.

'My word is my bond' has been the City's motto since 1801. That maxim helped to build the Square Mile's wealth and reputation, and it made business simple to transact. But how true is that today? Can all parties really be trusted to complete a deal when they have given their word alone? And when they have committed themselves to a course of action, will they stay the course, whatever the personal consequences?

It is sobering to realize that when the Barings Bank first went bust in 1890 the partners (as they were) honoured all the bank's debts. A recent *Times* essay on the subject commented: 'It seems unlikely we shall have the same comforting result this time round.'[5]

Today is it not the case that negotiation can sometimes be more about what the players can get away with, or get past the regulator? So clients spend large sums on 'due diligence', and there are often more lawyers than principles in the negotiating room.

We lie on the phone or in a meeting in order to achieve results or because we are under pressure. 'Is that your best price?' was a question faced every day by one timber trader I know. He is a Christian, so when it *was* his best price, did he say 'yes', as he had to tell the truth (but miss the opportunity of bargaining higher)? Or did he say 'no' (and lie), because he had targets to meet and he sensed some more movement in the bidding?

e. Flattery

Flattery is another aspect of false testimony and is common in some work cultures. We can obviously damn colleagues or competitors with faint praise. But we can also devalue people by flattering them with excessive or false praise. Flattery is when we say to someone's face what we are not saying behind their back. It is insincere.

We should aim to value people by giving them honest, constructive feedback and show appreciation. My colleague recently commented that while I was encouraging it was often too general; what she wanted was much more specific feedback that she could act on. I was in danger of flattering her to compensate for her experience of previous critical managers, but this wasn't helping her at all.

Conversely, we are more valuable to our managers when we refrain from flattering them. There is nothing to be gained from being surrounded by fawning courtiers and yes men. An *FT* reader once wrote in with a reminder of how to stand up to a press baron by recalling scenes from Evelyn Waugh's novel *Scoop*: whenever Lord Copper's secretary agreed with him he would say, 'Definitely, Lord Copper'. When his boss was talking rubbish, he'd respond: 'Up to a point, Lord Copper'. Very helpful advice!

f. Briefing (usually the press)

Financial PR is a powerful weapon in the workings of the markets. Practitioners can be economical with the truth or even mislead. How they brief is important, as the press and PR industry have a great responsibility and huge influence. They are often the 'prophets' of our generation.

Sometimes telling the truth, but at an inappropriate time or in an inappropriate way, is tantamount to being a false witness. It is a weapon often used by rivals, especially political rivals. The tactic of briefing journalists with unattractive but correct truth about a rival can be very damaging, perhaps by revealing a past affair or involvement in an incident for which the individual has already been punished. It can be just as serious as briefing with wrong or misleading information.

g. Research/analysts' opinions

In the relationship between analysts and brokers, commercial interest can at times impinge on the apparent independence of a research report or an analyst's opinion. One may ask whether the dot.com bubble in the US would have occurred, or would have occurred to the same extent, if analysts who thought that the stock was poor had been given the freedom to state their opinions honestly. Many ordinary investors got hurt in the fallout.

When I was a partner in a large property firm, one year I had responsibility for restructuring the research department. Was it to remain, as perceived in many quarters, as an ivory tower but safe within its walls of independence? Or were the constituent teams to be dispersed to work alongside their broking colleagues, in order to understand them better? Most of the brokers had a preference for closer working, so most of them went off, but some were to fall victim to their colleagues' enthusiasm to sell their own particular products.

John Kay stated in the *FT*: 'There should be less equity research, of higher quality, focused on market position and strategic direction rather than market tittle-tattle.'[6] He argued that the big investors must force change. I don't disagree with that, but each individual must also take responsibility for truth-telling.

h. Evidence

This commandment uses the language of the courtroom. Perjury undermines a case, it is corrosive to public trust in the system and is taken very seriously, as Jonathan Aitken discovered.[7] Incidentally, by the time he went to prison he was a changed man, as I found out when he was a helper in my Alpha group at that time. His faith and humility had a profound effect on the whole group.

In my own line of work I often have to give evidence at public inquiries. But although I am giving my own opinion as an expert, I am actually presenting my client's case in a form of advocacy, rather than as a truly independent witness.

i. Corporate cultures

The acid atmosphere of lies and deceit affects all our relationships, not just at home but particularly at work. Staff no longer believe their employers, and management is assumed to be pulling the wool over their eyes, breeding cynicism, contempt and fear. All *healthy* relationships are founded on openness and trust. So is it more than a coincidence that this epidemic of lying has also been an unprecedented time of breakdown in relationships, as seen by the failure of marriages, the disintegration of families, and increasing aloneness? At work we behave more and more as if we believe nothing and are prepared to say anything. It's just words, isn't it?

I once befriended the grandson of a man who during his lifetime had been known simply as Gibbo. He started work as a lowly clerk to Mr Selfridge, and the story goes that one day Gordon Selfridge was in the office when Gibbo took a call. 'It's for you, Mr Selfridge,' said Gibbo. 'Tell him I'm out,' replied Mr Selfridge. 'Tell him yourself,' said Gibbo and handed him the phone. It was a difficult moment! When Mr Selfridge put down the phone, Gibbo explained: 'If I can lie to him, I can lie to you.' With that one act he won his boss over and went on to become one of the most trusted members of that organization.

Choices

When we choose to say or do the right thing, often alone and in the face of much pressure, something happens in the heavenlies. We don't know how it will be used. When we act or say something when circumstances demand it, we also send a message to those around us, whether they are for us or against us. We also offer encouragement to those who are looking to do or say the right thing, but so far have felt under pressure not to do so.

We must not let anyone convince us that we have no power to make a difference. One person with one word or one action can make a difference – because God loves obedience and he uses it to act, and together we have the power to change whole organizations, even whole markets.

David Pickford, a great Christian who died not long ago, was a hero of mine. He was chairman of Haslemere, one of the most respected property developers in the business. He always spoke the truth with grace to everyone, so that his whole organization was imbued with it. The difference was clear to all, even in the way the phone was answered.

Those who lead organizations have a particular opportunity to affect their whole business. John D. Beckett, author of *Loving Monday* and *Making Monday*, is such a man of integrity and truth. His books tell the story of his desire to follow Jesus in his workplace and the effects this has had on his business and employees.

Words of truth

At the heart of the problem of bearing false witness is the problem of the human heart. Jesus puts the matter succinctly when he says, 'For out of the overflow of [a person's] heart his mouth speaks' (Luke 6:45). What comes out reflects what's inside us. We lie because:

- We are afraid, so we fight;
- We are exposed, so we cover up;
- We are hurt, so we retaliate;
- We are proud, so we put ourselves in a better light;
- We are self-centred, so we gain for ourselves, even if someone else loses.

In contrast, the Bible reveals God's character. God is true and there is nothing false in him. He is personal rather than some true force; not relative or just true for me or for those who follow him. No, logically, if he's true, he's true for us all.

Jesus came, 'full of grace and truth' (John 1:14). When we look at his life, deeds and teaching, we see God. This is what God is *like*. The apostle Peter said of him: 'He committed no sin, and no deceit was found in his mouth' (1 Peter 2:22). That speaks of *how* we say things, as well as *what* we say – like David Pickford.

If lying is endemic in our work culture, Jesus shows us how to live counterculturally: to forgive those who persecute us and not to do the same as them; to speak the truth in love, not with flattery or false words; to express righteous anger but not to hurt others; to expose hypocrisy but not to live by it; to accept others, whatever their background; and to turn the other cheek and not hit back.

Just as the Ten Commandments are set in the context of Israel's liberation from slavery, so Jesus leads people out of bondage to freedom, from death to life, and out of darkness into light.

Love in action

So how can we respond to God's love as expressed in this command? How might we cooperate with him and cultivate his life in us and in our workplace in the twenty-first century? I suggest six ways of demonstrating love in action.

1. Be filled with the truth

When Jesus was being tried on the testimony of a number of false witnesses, he was questioned by Pilate as to his kingship. Jesus had this to say to him, and to us: 'For this reason I was born, and for this reason I came into the world, to testify to the truth. Everyone on the side of truth listens to me.' 'What is truth?' Pilate asked (John 18:37–38). Pilate thought he was being so clever with this question, and it's the same clever question being asked in the media every day.

If we listen to the world, we will hear the voice of Pilate, and very soon we too will be washing our hands of the consequences of our own words. The most effective way of combatting lies is to fill our lives with truth: truth about God. By studying the life, person and teaching of Jesus every day and giving time to prayer, we maintain a living relationship with him.

2. Maintain restraint

The tongue is very powerful. Jesus' brother James described it as 'a restless evil, full of deadly poison' (James 3:8). He says it is like the rudder of a ship which, although tiny, can steer the course and set the direction.

Aesop, of the fables, was asked what was the most powerful thing in the world. He replied, 'The tongue'. And then he was asked what is the most harmful thing in the world. Again he replied, 'The tongue'. Words pop out before we realize it. We cannot retrieve them, and then we realize that we can never really undo the consequences. The damage has been done. Before we join in a conversation we should consider the merits of taking part at all. We don't *have* to join in. It's wise to weigh up the consequences of doing so and of what we might say.

The most effective way to avoid gossip is simply to restrain ourselves and not join in. It is much harder to get out of such a situation once you are in, even if at first you have to put up with a few jibes. We *can* stop. We *can* make a difference by not taking part, and this creates a momentum for others to stop too. If pressed, we could find something else to do, or even leave the room if possible. But sometimes we might just have to say something appropriate (but not preachy).

3. Practise truth-telling

Jesus said, 'Be as shrewd as snakes and as innocent as doves' (Matthew 10:16). We need to be smart about how we go about telling the truth, lest we be taken as naïve, as I once was many years ago. My senior partner tracked down a rumour (which happened to be true) to my secretary. I was called in as it was assumed that I had told her (because Christians tell the truth!). I explained that I hadn't revealed the matter, as it was highly confidential, and that although I was indeed truthful I was certainly not daft.

Returning to the timber trader I mentioned earlier, who was asked almost every day: 'Is that your best price?', how is he to respond? I suggested that he might find a response that is true to himself – not to lie (as that's wrong), but not necessarily to say yes if that's simply bad negotiation. Jesus often responded to a tricky question with another question. So the timber merchant might reply, 'Is that your best offer?!' It puts the issue back to the other person. Or he could use an expression that suits his personality, such as: 'Oh Harry, would I tell you that?' Or just laugh!

I would suggest that each of us should examine what is the equivalent question for ourselves – whatever it is that puts us on the spot – and come up with a form of response that is true to our personality *and* to the facts.

What stops us easily telling the truth? We need to be determined to be people of our word. Because when we tell the truth it makes a difference, even if it's just to us at first. But we also need to be smart in how we do it.

4. Confront lies (nicely)

This need not be done in an aggressive way and certainly not piously. A challenge can simply be a question. When you hear some snippet, you can ask, 'Is that the whole story?' Or 'Are you sure?' Gibbo's response to Mr Selfridge was challenging, yet not aggressive or direct.

If the gossiper persists, you may well have to bail out with 'I'm sorry, I would rather we didn't discuss so and so' or 'I am going to have to let go of this one; this is not for me.'

We stop by stopping, not by preaching. And if we stop we can break the cycle and encourage others to do the same.

5. Be an encourager

Cultivate a habit of positive talking, of being an encourager. This is a great reinforcer of honesty, and we are far less likely to fall into situations where we talk *against* others if our habit is always to speak about people positively.

But we too need encouragement. Meeting with other Christians to pray and for support is essential in the work environment. I have found this to be a vital part of my Christian life midweek. I have drawn encouragement from two main sources: a midweek talk of some sort, and a monthly prayer session with someone who understands the issues I am facing.

6. Cultivate regular forgiveness

We will all fail from time to time – of that we can be sure. The trick is to get up quickly, confess our failure to God and move on in the freedom that comes from being forgiven. Staying down is disheartening, even debilitating.

It is also good not to let stuff fester. If we have wronged someone by what we have said, then we should put it right with them directly. I worked with a man who, though a committed Christian, allowed all sorts of issues to go un-resolved. It affected his whole demeanour and had a corrosive effect on his relationships.

I once mediated between two colleagues whose relation-ship broke down when they got stuck on a project. It was too important to the consultancy to let it go. After allowing each of them to get their opinions off their chest, we began to explore the background to their views of each other. The younger had had a bad experience of a domineering boss, and had responded to this colleague with similar reactions. Once he had apologized the relationship changed, and they were able to resolve their differences and establish a basis for working together with mutual respect.

Live counterculturally

How are we to live the countercultural life that Jesus offers? How are we to cooperate with him, to allow his character to seep through, and to be honest?

We do this by being people of truth: by absorbing God's truth through daily study of his Word and through prayer; by allowing him to work in us so that we can indeed forgive, rather than persecute; by speaking truth in love and not out of flattery; by speaking out with strength when necessary; by exposing hypocrisy with love while not living it; and by turning the other cheek when we are insulted – in short, by breaking the cycle of lies in order to see change.

For reflection

1. Do you find it hard to resist joining in with gossip? Why?
2. What do colleagues say about you when you try not to join in? How do you deal with that?

3. Is there a common question in your work (like the example of the timber trader) that you find difficult to answer? How might you answer it differently tomorrow?
4. If you are accused of some failure, how do you react?
5. How can you cultivate the habit of always answering positively when asked your opinion about a colleague?

3. PROSPERING WITH INTEGRITY

You shall not steal.
(Exodus 20:15)

We start by taking the towels from the hotel, or we adjust our expenses. We may regard taking a few items off the shelves or from the stores as acceptable; work's stationery is a perk – paper, CDs, cartridges, pens, even petty cash (to repay those occasions when work has cost us); or it could be software. Does it really matter that these things are not ours?

Such 'minor' theft is happening on an epidemic scale.

The results of a KPMG survey reported in *Human Resources Magazine* revealed that 28% of managers and employees had *seen* colleagues steal stocks or supplies, 27% *knew* of staff who fiddled expenses and 23% had *seen* money stolen.[1]

This is nothing new of course. One national newspaper ran a lead story with the headline: 'Britain: a nation of cheats and thieves', based on a survey on theft in the workplace.[2] It was found that three quarters of all Britons steal from their employers, a quarter will *create* opportunities to steal, and half of us *will* steal where the opportunity arises.

We may start small but we don't know where it will end. Wal-Mart forced the resignation of a Board Director over allegations that up to $500,000 were obtained through unauthorized use of company gift cards and false expense reports.

Fear of theft

We have locks on everything: our offices, homes, cars, even our phones. You would not dream of leaving your stuff lying about. In fact the City of London now has a level of camera surveillance that was once reserved for prisons. Computer passwords are just the lowest level of security to counter sophisticated remote hackers. Levels of ID fraud are such that we are wary of cash machines and of leaving unshredded utility bills in our rubbish.

If we all took the eighth commandment seriously, it has the potential totally to transform our lives, which are now so dominated by security, crime and fear of crime.

As with all the commandments, this is about more than lifestyle and our actions: it is about our inner lives and the effect of this activity on our very souls. Again, God is setting out this boundary in order to protect us. He does this out of his deep love and concern for us. He knows our vulnerability and fragility. As with the breaking of any of the other commandments, he knows the consequences only too well. We start with small things and the habit grows. And it offends God, hurts us and damages others.

While this commandment is, at face value, a prohibition against stealing anything at any time under any circumstances, it is so much more than mere protection of other people's possessions. Yes, there is an obvious impact of stealing on the life of any community, and the community will punish the transgressor, but the essential feature is that the transgressor loses not only freedom (both temporal and spiritual) but the presence of God.

Through the work of Jesus on the cross and the life-giving Holy Spirit, God is doing a work in those who believe in him. He is moving in our hearts to obey him, not out of obligation but out of love. In the language of a promise this commandment says, 'You will not even want to steal; you have no appetite for it, no desire at all.'

Stealing

Stealing is taking something that is rightfully someone else's. The prohibition of stealing is a generally accepted standard in virtually all the world's cultures, where the basis may often be the simple protection of individual property rights. In God's economy, however, it also involves the protection of ourselves *from* ourselves – that is, it has more to do with our inner life than our outward behaviour, important as that is.

Rooted in the culture

The scandal of MPs' expenses was not so much about the criminality of the parliamentarians but the culture that had been allowed to grow up around their rewards. So instead of better pay (which had been held down to appease voters), MPs were 'allowed' to claim for all sorts of things on expenses to compensate. So they did.

The same can happen in all organizations and at all levels. The key is to examine the culture. Look to see what is 'allowed' to happen: whether it's dodgy accounting principles, letting contracts to friends and relatives, preferential share deals or whatever. Like the MPs, we don't go into work intending to steal, but we can easily get absorbed into the culture of the place. And it's infectious.

In 2009 Mr Puddick discovered his wife was having an affair with her boss Mr Haynes. Mr Puddick's subsequent trial for harassment of his wife's lover in 2011 brought this matter to public attention, although he was acquitted. But what caught my attention was how this affair was financed. *The Times* explained: 'Even after her husband learnt of the affair, Mr Haynes wanted to continue their relationship, which he funded by fraudulently claiming company expenses, Mrs Puddick told the court.' It went on: 'She also admitted helping her boss to fabricate his expenses claims to ensure that he did not have personally to pay for wining and dining her. "He did not have to put his hand in his own pocket," she said. "I would ask him 'What should I fill in?' He would give me a client name. That was the culture."[3]

Back in the heady post-war days of Clydeside shipbuilding, when there were 500 wage-rates in John Brown's yard alone and all got the sack once the ship was completed, ships were built mainly at weekends, on overtime. Half the workers did not turn up on Mondays and Tuesdays. But one of the main perks, hallowed by tradition, was pilfering. During the troubled construction of the QE2 in the 1960s, *The Times* reported that 'Many a Clydeside house was proudly equipped with QE2 doorknobs and a patch of pink, puce and plum carpet from the main ballroom.'[4] Again, it was part of the culture.

Variety

In a work context there are a surprising number of ways in which we can steal:

a. Dishonesty

We may fill out our expenses accurately, but was that our client or our friend we entertained? A friend of mine runs a business where entertaining is expensive, but he always has to keep tabs on who his staff are entertaining! Or we may promise delivery deadlines we cannot hope to meet, thereby causing financial loss to the other party. If we charge for things we are not entitled to, maybe billing more hours than we actually logged, we are being dishonest (even if the client pays). Selling goods or services for more than they are worth is also effectively stealing. Filling in a loan application based on false information can lead to gaining money that we have no hope of repaying. Similarly, filing an insurance claim that is excessive or plain dishonest is tantamount to stealing.

b. Sickies

The chairman of one organization was asked: 'How many people work here?' He replied, 'About half'. One of the most practised forms of theft in our working environment involves *time*. Taking time off, ostensibly due to illness, amounts to leave without due authorization. Sickies steal time from our employers, and that costs them money. When we take a sickie or bunk off work early, we are being paid for not working. In other words we are taking what is not rightfully ours, and that is stealing.

The average British worker takes off seven days a year. Sickies became such a problem at the Royal Mail, where individual workers were taking on average twelve days' sick leave each year, that an incentive scheme called 'Be in to win' was introduced and workers were rewarded with new cars and holiday vouchers if they did not take sick leave. £500,000 worth of goods had already been given away when I came across this scheme.

But what about when our bosses insist on us working late beyond reasonable expectations and without extra pay, often outside contractual obligations? This practice may be endemic to the culture of an organization. Are they stealing from us? Robbing us of *our* time?

c. Defaulting on loans or obligations

This can include failing to honour obligations by defaulting on repayment of a loan, or perhaps a liquidation that could have been avoided, leaving people out of work. Or what about the common occurrence of a company being placed in administration, whereby debts are cancelled and the original owner can buy back the company without even ceasing trading?

We could include here the practice of deliberately not returning things we have borrowed: how many books have been loaned to me and never returned?

Some of this activity is quite subtle: contractual obligations to pay a supplier within thirty days are extended, sometimes to months, and not always by powerful buyers. Quite often this leads to financial hardship for the other party. It may be legal, but perhaps this too could be seen as a form of theft.

d. Deception and misrepresentation: false promises

This includes financial products that are 'mis-sold', software that is pirated, shares offered in a company that can't fulfil its promises, or goods and services that don't live up to their description. All of this can lead to someone else's financial loss. But the book of Proverbs says, 'The LORD detests differing weights, and dishonest scales do not please him' (20:23).

e. Defrauding

VAT evasion is an art form in some quarters, but we also defraud the government when we don't pay our taxes (it is not a sport to win at, as some would advocate). Tax evasion costs us all and results in lower tax receipts of nearly £20 billion a year. It is not our job to redesign the country's tax system or to decide what rate of tax we should pay! Jesus said, 'Give to Caesar what is Caesar's and to God what is God's' (Mark 12:17).

Or we can defraud businesses by downloading software that should be paid for, for example: often software that we have obtained at work.

f. Money laundering

This may not be stealing directly, but it's possible to participate in some way, perhaps due to complacency. Britain's efforts to combat money laundering were described as 'pathetic' by a world expert on financial crime. So we do what we can by complying with the often tedious procedures of the banks and other authorities.

g. Bribery

When a corrupt security guard takes money from you to let you pass, he has just stolen from you. When a procurement officer allows a contract as a result of a bribe, he has stolen from the deserving winner.

h. Fraud

We don't have to walk out of the building with money to be stealing. In February 1995 I was in Singapore with a colleague. One evening we were waiting for our hosts – a property developer and his lawyer wife – at their country club. She was very late, so late in fact that she missed most of the meal. When she finally appeared, she explained that she had been called in by the authorities: a young trader no-one had heard of had just knocked a huge hole in a British investment bank – someone called Leeson, she said. The next day the papers carried the story, and we have all heard of Nick Leeson and the fate of Barings Bank.

Investment scams can thrive in an environment where there is so much money to be made. Mr Madoff seems to have been a respectable broker until he got greedy and started his Ponzi scheme, the largest in history. Many people lost out. I read how Wood Green Crown Court had jailed a conman called Rich, ironically, who persuaded his victims to part with millions in an investment scam. He ended up with £10 in his

Sainsbury's bank account after being duped out of his ill-gotten gains by another conman.

Too much is not enough

I came across this extraordinary piece of research: in the US, researchers linked the size of bosses' stock options with their willingness to commit fraud and found that the value of stock options granted to the CEOs of firms which committed fraud was 800% greater than those granted to the CEOs of firms not guilty of any wrongdoing. *The Economist* commented: 'Nothing correlated so strongly with corporate fraud as the value of stock options – not the standard of the firm's governance, nor analysts' inflated expectations about their earnings, nor ego-boosting stories about their CEOs in the press.'[5] Even too much was not enough.

Words

In all this activity we use a sea of words to cover our guilt, such as:

- Mis-described
- Mis-sold
- Adjusted
- Recycled
- Over-optimistic
- Misappropriated
- Inaccurate
- Unexplained
- Surplus

Our heart matters

As ever, the heart of this problem is spiritual. When we read of cases in the press, such as Michael Rich or the more high-profile Bernie Ebbers, it is usually that they became gripped by one of the two great motivators of the marketplace: greed or fear.

Notice that in breaking the eighth commandment it is difficult to avoid breaking the tenth – not to covet. They are often linked, so if we overcome our covetousness we reduce the risk of stealing.

Money has become an *idol* for many. And of course idols are worshipped. Money can be a good servant, but it is a bad master. Jesus said, 'No servant can serve two masters. Either he will hate one and love the other, or he will be devoted to one and despise the other. You cannot serve both God and Money' (Luke 16:13). Yet some of us try to lead compartmentalized lives.

It's not that God has a 'down' on money; it's just that he knows its power. He is not against us making money; rather he wants to liberate us from its power when we do so. He wants us to prosper – but with a clear conscience, and with integrity. The great virtue of Job, a man of immense wealth, was his integrity (see Job 2:3, 9).

God also wants to liberate us from the power of possessions. Ironically, those things that we consume ultimately consume *us*. We think we have possessions, but they actually possess us. They cling to us as we cling to them. But the simple truth is they are not ours anyway! We have a false understanding of possessions. The liberating truth of the Bible is that everything ultimately belongs to God. We are stewards not owners, tenants not landlords. King David, at the height of his wealth and power, wrote: 'Everything comes from you, and we have given you only what comes from your hand' (1 Chronicles 29:14). No wonder God called David a man after his own heart (1 Samuel 13:14)!

All forms of stealing are toxic. But what is the antidote? Our response is to allow God to work in our heart. How might we cooperate with him and live a fulfilled working life? The answer is to respond to the initiatives that God has already taken.

In his very practical and readable book *You Can Change*, Tim Chester explains that we need help: 'I need someone to change me. Trying to imitate Jesus on its own only leaves me feeling a failure. I can't be like him. I can't match up. I need rescuing. I need forgiveness.'[6] He goes on to explain that Jesus came to make us into God's image; that God is transforming us so that we are no longer motivated by the fear of the law, but by the opportunity to experience glory. We become who we are in Christ. 'The challenge,' says Tim, 'is to let these new identities define us on Monday mornings.'

Responding to God's initiative

I want to outline six ways in which we can live under grace, not under law, and act out our cooperation with the living God whom we serve and who works in us more than we can ask or imagine.

1. Go for brutal honesty

No techniques will work unless we face what is really going on in our hearts. We have to face the facts. And often the most difficult person to face is our very self. Our hearts are deceitful, so we need to be brutally honest with ourselves before we can be honest with others. We may need the help of a minister, a friend, a trusted colleague or a counsellor to help us face what is going on and bring any issues into the light.

We must also be brutally honest with God, because only God can truly change our hearts. We need to come to him and confess our sin, with the amazing result that, as we repent and receive forgiveness, we are set free. It's a hugely liberating experience, and we will walk away so much lighter.

2. Practise restitution

The eighth commandment is one of the few where we can make amends for something we have done wrong, and putting things right is a powerful experience.

Making amends is one of the early steps in a twelve-step programme adopted by those battling alcoholism and addiction, and I have seen how effective it can be for someone not just to face what they have done wrong, but to put it right, as far as it is in their power to do so. I was privileged to help a recovering alcoholic take a particular step. He had recently found that the 'Higher Power' that had helped him thus far was in fact Jesus. Before I went through this step with him, he told me about how he had let a lot of people down along the way. He had written to them all, as far as he could remember, and tried to put things right. I saw how this can lead to positive help for the victims and also contributes to the healing of the one who has wronged them.

Jesus had an encounter with Zacchaeus, a senior tax collector for the occupying forces based in Jericho (Luke 19:1–9). He was a small, wealthy man who was loathed by his own people, but was shown love and acceptance by Jesus. When Jesus came back to his house, Zacchaeus stood up before his peers and announced that he was going to give half his possessions to the poor and that he would give back to any he had cheated four times the amount they had lost. In this statement he was expressing his repentance and desire for restitution. Jesus' response was: 'Today salvation has come to this house' (Luke 19:9).

Perhaps you need to take similar action. It might mean honouring a commitment, painful though that may be. Or if we have taken anything at all from our workplace, we should give it back as soon as we can. It could be money, stationery or something much bigger.

3. Exercise a thankful heart

A strong antidote to greed is thankfulness: to thank God for what we have received. Covetousness robs us of what we already have, as we saw when looking at the tenth commandment. Giving thanks for what we have acts as a drag on the process of wanting something else, and it helps to stop the corrosion of allowing the wanting to lead, ultimately, to taking.

We all have something to thank God for: for our very lives, for our family, our relationships, the kind of work we do, our livelihoods . . . For Jesus knows that where our treasure is, there our heart will be too (Matthew 6:21).

4. Keep on giving it away

The most effective way to defeat the desire to take is by giving. A thankful heart is more likely to lead to a giving heart. And there is nothing quite like giving away what you have in order to curb unhealthy appetites for money and wealth. This is an act of will: a decision. If we hold things lightly, they are less likely to take hold of us.

Robert Edmiston, the founder of IM Group, the car importer, has said that before he dies he hopes to give away £300 million of his £352 million personal fortune. He admits he will nevertheless remain in a more financially privileged position than many. But he is letting go of an awful lot. John Wesley, preaching in the eighteenth century, expressed this godly attitude succinctly: 'Own all you can; save all you can; give all you can.'

Sometimes we need practical help: just donating to a charity can seem impersonal and detached from our hearts.

A friend of mine, James Odgers, started a charity known as The Besom to help donors. James was a successful lawyer and banker, so perhaps he knows the hearts of such people! He finds that people appreciate the opportunity to give and also to know how their giving has made a difference. His charity has helped many to give of their money, time or possessions, and in a way that keeps the donors' hearts involved by supplying progress reports on how the money has been spent and the impact this had had on people's lives.

Some people tithe (though what that means is a whole topic in itself!) or establish some other way of ensuring that they give away a proportion of their earnings. Unless we prioritize our giving, we will often find it doesn't happen. My wife and I set up a Tithe account, and a standing order each month ensures that money goes out to others.

5. Maintain integrity

In this commandment God promises that we can leave the tools in the store, the stationery at work, minimize personal calls, fill in our expenses honestly and so enjoy freedom! If we obey in all the small things then it's easier with the bigger temptations. It may not always win us friends or earn us respect. But it's the right thing to do.

I heard of one employee in the Civil Service who decided that he would no longer photocopy private documents at work or make personal calls on the office phone. He would do these things outside the office or not at all. This started to have an effect on others, and over time his superiors noticed that his department was spending less on such items and had become more efficient and motivated.

None of us is totally alone in our work. Many of us are part of an organization, or if we are self-employed we have customers or suppliers, and so we all have individual responsibility. We can use that opportunity to support good practices and initiatives, so that honesty and integrity extend to all our activities, whether they are credit control practices, buying policies, dealings with Third World countries or environmental policy.

We can each play our part and when we do so we open the door for God to become involved.

6. Cultivate a 'daily bread' lifestyle

So many of us got caught up in the boom years: we lived for tomorrow, which was always going to be better. Now the UK has double the level of debt of our European neighbours. And that debt can add to our fears.

We will not survive well in this environment, nor will we change it, without turning back to God and relying on him. We *can* be content, even now, but it will mean being content with 'enough'. When we pray the words that Jesus himself taught us: 'Give us this day our daily bread', what does that mean in practice? The book of Proverbs gives us this insightful explanation:

> Give me neither poverty nor riches,
>   but give me only my daily bread.
> Otherwise, I may have too much and disown you
>   and say, 'Who is the LORD?'
> Or I may become poor and steal,
>   and so dishonour the name of my God.
> (Proverbs 30:8–9)

Enough is enough

The great lie is *More*. But the great secret is *Enough*. Each of us has to determine before God what that is for ourselves. But the truth is that both too much and too little money are bad for us. The secret is enough: our daily bread. If we can cultivate a life that is based on trusting in God and his provision rather than our own, we will find we can prosper with integrity, give to our neighbour, find contentment and avoid taking what belongs to another.

For reflection

1. Are there any 'small' items that you find yourself taking from work? Do you have difficulty being totally honest in claiming expenses, filling in your tax return or avoiding 'sickies'? What can you do to clean up your act?
2. Have you ever put misleading or false information on a form?
3. How good – and consistent – are you in your giving?
4. Do you have *Enough*? What does that mean for you?

4. MAINTAINING HEALTHY RELATIONSHIPS

You shall not commit adultery.
(Exodus 20:14)

As human beings we crave intimacy, and many find this in the workplace. Both the overt and subtle influences of the workplace shape the depth and quality of the intimacy we experience at work. For many, relationships will be healthy but this is not always the case. The workplace can offer many different kinds of opportunities for intimacy, depending on the nature and context of our work, and this can present challenges for both single and married people.

Andrew and Nada Kakabadse carried out a survey: 'Intimacy: International Survey of the Sex Lives of People at Work'.[1] The research was primarily carried out by in-depth interviews, face to face. Of the 221 people interviewed,

- 60% admitted to having experienced emotional or physical intimacy at work;
- 31% admitted to both;
- 8% admitted to physical intimacy alone.

The study highlighted that people work better when they are enjoying an intimate relationship, and so extrapolated that there are positive benefits of intimacy in the office: 'From an organisational perspective these relationships are very positive because they make people more committed to the employer. If the relationship goes wrong, people may be hurt but there's no mechanism for preventing that kind of hurt.'

Encouraging such a level of intimacy in the workplace is a high-risk approach. The mechanism for preventing that kind of hurt is to establish clear boundaries to intimacy. That is what God is doing with his gift of this commandment. Marriage is intended to be the ultimate experience of human intimacy. Society, employers and we as individuals, whether married or single, all have a role in helping to support and uphold marriage. The Bible does not encourage us to replace marriage with something less.

Outdated?

Why should this commandment – with such apparently limited application to the workplace – be relevant to us today?

I believe it is utterly foundational. First, because the workplace affords the opportunity to support healthy marriages and relationships. But secondly, it also addresses a threat to healthy relationships.

The workplace is often a social setting and so a primary place for forming relationships, which is good. Workplaces that foster healthy relationships can also be places of real fulfilment and blessing. Given the right circumstances they can be places where marriages and healthy relationships are valued, appreciated, supported and safeguarded, but much depends on the prevailing culture.

But work can also be a tricky place. It might be a place where single people are expected to behave inappropriately, even promiscuously; or it might simply be a place where men often 'play away', particularly if travelling on business. More likely the threat is far less overt. Perhaps a single person and a married colleague spend so much time together that all too easily an unhelpful attachment forms. And if the marriage has not been nurtured, this can even lead to an affair.

The pressures of work itself, coupled with excessive hours spent in the workplace, can pose a threat to relationships and leave us with little time or energy to invest in, or form, healthy relationships outside of work. Stress, worry and fear at work can all impact upon a marriage and our ability to form healthy friendships. Other activities such as after-office entertainments can also throw up temptations to extra-marital relationships or even affairs.

Protecting marriage

God has given marriage as a special lifelong partnership of love between a man and a woman, with commitment at the heart of it and with one unique expression of that commitment: a sexual relationship. Because of his deep love for us, and knowing our weakness, God wants to protect us from hurt and guilt in marriage and to guard others from the fallout from broken or damaging relationships.

Adultery denies love, degrades people, destroys families, defiles marriage and defies God. Given this potential for distortion and its destructive power, this commandment seeks to put a restraint on one of the most powerful forces within us, namely our sex drive. In reviewing the vow of chastity, historically one of the church's responses to sexual temptation, Richard Foster comments: 'It reminds us that discipline and denial are gospel imperatives. You see, our sexual intoxication is only representative of an all-pervasive mood of intemperance that dominates the world in which we live today.'[2]

God has not got a 'down' on sex. He is not a grumpy old man in the sky looking down on us and muttering, 'Whatever will they get up to next?!' No, God actually invented sex: it was his idea. Three chapters of the book of Proverbs are devoted to it, and the Song of Songs has overt sexual themes. However, God is very realistic about the dangers of sex, for he knows its power and our human weakness. Sex needs boundaries and a context, so in his love for us, God has placed constraints around it for our protection.

Alternative perspectives

Not everyone in our culture has such a serious view of marriage and the impact of adultery. A few years ago the BBC reviewed the place of adultery in our culture in a TV series entitled *Heaven and Earth*. One episode found lust to be the sin most of us enjoy (41% of men and 26% of women), though apparently more women enjoy gluttony than men do! In the new popular rankings adultery got downgraded. The presenter Ross Kelly explained, 'Attitudes to sin have changed . . . While many of us actually enjoy lust, we still frown on adultery.' The tragedy is that so many people really believe that they can indulge in the one without it leading to the other.

In Channel 4's *The New Ten Commandments*, broadcast at about the same time, this commandment only narrowly made it into the top twenty at eighteenth place.

A covenant relationship

At face value this commandment is a straightforward prohibition against sex outside marriage. In the culture in which it was given, the punishment for violation of the commandment was usually death. John Durham explains it like this:

> This attitude toward adultery is fully understandable only in view of the fact that more than the integrity of marriage and the home . . . were at stake in the covenantal relationship . . . Adultery with the husband or wife betrothed of another was, like idol worship, a turning away from commitment to Yahweh.[3]

For Christians, marriage is more than an institution or a relationship option. It is the joining of two people spiritually: 'For this reason a man will leave his father and mother and be united to his wife, and they will become one flesh' (Genesis 2:24). Sexual intimacy is at the heart of that oneness – it means becoming one flesh in the context of marriage, for the rest of our lives, and that is why sex can't be casual.

Adultery is a betrayal of trust. It's a most serious wound to a marriage and can often be fatal. As with each commandment, this one is designed by a loving God for our protection – as much for ourselves as for our spouse and all the others who get hurt when a marriage fails. Adultery has far-reaching consequences that can cause much relational pain and damage. Marriage is at the heart of family, and the family is the basic building block of society, so this issue is important to us all.

In a *Sunday Times Magazine* article, Susan Greenhill wrote about how infidelity wrecks lives, including her own:

> My story is not unusual. When I married at 22 I had a great job in television. A few years down the line, I was a full-time mother with three young children. My family seemed in need of a servant – and I was it. When their lives constantly expanded, mine seemed only to contract. It was like being in a long tunnel and not being able to see the end. My husband was working hard and had less and less time for me. My confidence dropped. I felt socially inadequate. I grew restless. Then I met a young freelance copywriter who, unlike my hardworking husband, had plenty of time to spend with me.[4]

It led to an affair which didn't last. She was soon alone, with three children to care for, struggling to find another relationship and feeling guilty about what she had done to her family.

Susan Greenhill commented: 'Affairs are selfish.' Marriage is about giving, whereas adultery is about taking.

Freedom within boundaries

One of the main reasons why relationships are in turmoil is because we have turned the nature of freedom inside out. Our culture thinks freedom is to be found *beyond* boundaries, equating freedom with liberation. But God's way is to allow us to enjoy sexual freedom within boundaries. By observing this seventh commandment, married couples can enjoy the security that allows for vulnerability and intimacy, and the warmth of mutual love and real sexual freedom within the boundaries of a lifelong, loving relationship. It provides firm foundations for raising children and also protects those boundaries which are so vital for the development of trust and intimacy.

So this commandment is all about protecting marriages because marriage is very important to God. But it is relevant to singles too and to the whole of society. Marriage has always been under threat. That threat comes mostly from within our own hearts – for example, when we are tempted into an extra-marital relationship. This hurts both us and others, as well as God. Hence the tenth commandment remains so important – not to covet what is not ours.

Being squeezed into the world's mould

Marriage is also under threat from increasingly strong cultural influences all around us:

Consumerism

Consumerism breeds a tendency to dispose of the old and acquire the new. In this process I no longer appreciate what I have because something better has become available. We see this with mobile phones, laptops, computer games and other gadgets. In a fast-moving technological environment, it is increasingly cheaper to throw something away when it is broken, rather than get it mended. And the same attitude can affect our relationships. We don't fix them; we just get new ones. We don't hang in for the long haul; we cast off our spouse when we find a newer (and often younger) model.

Sexualization

Sex has become all-pervasive and is now inescapable: in TV programmes of almost every kind, films, music lyrics and videos, magazines and especially on the internet. One wonders what the advertising industry would do if sex hadn't been invented! We are submerged by sex. Series such as *Sex and the City* feed our workplace culture. Seduction and flirtation are portrayed by the media as romantic and fulfilling, and there is far less focus on the hurt, the shame and the wrecked lives. When did you last see a loving, sexually fulfilled relationship shown in the context of marriage?

The so-called sexual revolution was designed to bring liberty and fulfilment, but in reality it has brought us more enslavement and dissatisfaction. Today the worldwide pornography industry makes more money than the entire global car industry. An IT consultant I met recently commented that the internet, while helpful to business, does not run primarily for email and information, but is driven mainly by pornography.

But it is not so much that we think about sex too much, but rather that we have such a low view of it. Sex has been hijacked from its place in marriage and detached to become a stand-alone pleasure. Marriage is in decline and the consequences for society are dire. The knitting is unravelling.

Commoditization

The combination of consumerism and sexualization leads inevitably to commoditization, which affects how we view one another. We see people as objects, a view described by Pope John Paul II as 'utilitarian'. Advertising, TV, magazines and newspapers can all portray men and women as objects rather than as valued human beings. Messages tell us to conform to a certain image: cosmetic surgery will make you more confident; wear this and you will be successful; buy that product and you will be happy; drive that car and you will get more girlfriends.

Image is being valued over substance, and ultimately we see one another as objects rather than real people. That weakens men's view of women, leading in no small way to an increase in the use of pornography, which is fuelled by such easy internet access.

Emotional intellect

There seems to be a growing tendency for people to be motivated by their feelings rather than by their thinking, and we are increasingly at home with our feelings. Over a twenty-five-year period of leading small groups on the Alpha Course, I have noticed that the nature of small groups has changed. Twenty-five years ago I would have started the discussion with an open question, such as: 'What do you think?' Today that would be insufficient to engage more than half the group. Now I would have to follow it up, or open with: 'And what do you feel?' More and more people operate out of their feelings: what they feel is what they believe.

Of course feelings are notoriously unreliable; but if that is your operating mode (what I have called 'emotional intellect') then relying on feelings alone can lead to dire consequences. So if someone *feels* that they are no longer in love with their spouse, they can then quickly move to *believing* that they no longer love that person. And in a consumerist culture they move on.

Work culture

A generation or so ago I would have said that we took our home culture to work; but today we take our work culture home or into our personal relationships.

The signs of a home-based culture were paternalism and a rhythm and pace that was reasonably in tune with a home-based life (and a home life where children were brought up by a home-based mother). Not all of that was necessarily good of course, and I am not suggesting that we hark back to some 'golden age'.

Today most marriage partners will work, which itself has an impact on marriage and family life. That might simply be on account of long work hours, but increasingly we are taking our work culture home. This means that we adopt the cultural styles and practices of our workplaces. For example, I have *meetings* with my wife and schedule *appointments* to spend time with my children. I adopt styles of conflict resolution that are more corporate than domestic: I get to my point; I am in a hurry; I want results and quickly.

My wife and I help out on The Marriage Course. At the end of one course one couple came to see us, and it was apparent that they were struggling with the way in which they resolved conflict. After we had teased out some of the causes, the wife was quite shocked to realize that her tough, combative corporate approach to conflict resolution was coming home with her! And her husband was finding it quite difficult.

I now work in an office where the culture tends towards mockery of the Christian perspective (but interestingly is respectful of other faiths) and where the senior managers would not necessarily regard marriage as a positive thing, partly because of their own experiences, directly or indirectly. So speaking about these topics needs careful handling, particularly by me. I will explore some of the ways I do that later.

The work context

The workplace needs more champions for marriage and healthy relationships – from individuals and a supportive management or HR department which fosters family-friendly practices and policies. But what they do and say will not embed itself in the culture unless people are treated with respect. As one colleague commented to me at a recent strategy day, 'It's all very well having a corporate objective that values our staff, but it means we can't make them redundant every time the market changes.'

Marriage is often under attack, though the threat sometimes comes from further afield and is not always direct or obvious at work. For example:

- In the decreasing value given to marriage. I have noticed that cohabitation is seen as 'obviously' preferable, even as a precursor to marriage;
- In the way marriage is devalued in the workplace: for example, where workers who are prepared to spend more time at work are favoured over those who have spouses or children to go home to;
- In sexual behaviour before marriage;
- In attitudes to the value of sex;
- In the games people play at work, after work or when away on business.

Less obvious threats are those caused by wrong views of sex, and they come out in our conversation and attitudes, particularly at work. All too often this leads to a pervasive and corrosive effect on our work culture and business lives, and poverty of relationships in the workplace. Many are in pain.

Society's poor view of sex leads to a poor view of women (and men!) and gives rise to considerable distortions in workplace culture and relationships, so that we see discrimination against women in the form of unequal pay, abusive language, sexual harassment and pervasive sexism. This deep-seated problem was highlighted recently by a House of Commons Trade and Industry Select Committee. The City has seen a number of high-profile sex-discrimination cases, and while some of these cases were dismissed, an underlying sexist culture in the City seems to prevail.

Christian responses

It is important to say that it is not the church's position to be judgmental about broken relationships or sexual sin, though that is the impression often given. Christians can get very fussed about sex! It is a subject many of us find hard to deal with in a workplace setting, where very few share our beliefs. We become known for what we are against, rather than what we are for. We might be labelled as 'out of touch', 'homophobic', 'oppressive', 'puritanical' or even worse. We are seen as old-fashioned and out of tune with current attitudes, and our opinions are not valued, even if they have been expressed quite positively.

The example of Jesus

It's a great inspiration to see how Jesus dealt with the woman caught in adultery (John 8:1–11). This is one of my favourite passages. It shows just what God is like and how Jesus came with both grace and truth. It demonstrates his deep love and compassion for those who fall, and his ability to transmit the liberating truth of the gospel by *how* he deals with a situation.

In the eyewitness account John relates how the religious leaders brought to Jesus a woman described as 'caught in the act of adultery'. The incident occurred at dawn near the temple courts where people had gathered around to hear Jesus teach. How the religious leaders bundled this woman into the temple courts is not clear, but it's possible that she was scantily dressed and had been sleeping with someone who was not her husband. Notice that the man who had been enjoying her company was nowhere to be seen!

The religious leaders posed a question designed to trap Jesus: was this woman to be judged by the law as deserving of death? What would Jesus say? No doubt all the people gathered round him found it rather interesting to stare at this scantily dressed woman. But Jesus bent down and, rather than look at her, started to write on the ground with his finger. The religious leaders continued to question him. Still Jesus did not look at the woman but, stooping down, he wrote on the ground challenging the accusers and those with them: 'If any one of you is without sin, let him be the first to throw a stone at her.' One by one the people departed until Jesus was left alone with her.

Straightening up he asked her: 'Woman, where are they? Has no-one condemned you?' 'No-one, sir,' she said. Jesus replied, 'Then neither do I condemn you.' That is grace.

Jesus was full of love and compassion for this woman. At no point did he wag his finger at her or accuse her. And in that context of love he was able to say to her finally, 'Go now and leave your life of sin.' That is truth.

In this story we see that God is in the business of demon-strating his love and grace to us, yet freeing us of the sin in our lives. If only the church – you and me – could be like this at work!

An issue of the heart

Jesus said, 'You have heard that it was said: "Do not commit adultery." But I tell you that anyone who looks at a woman lustfully has already committed adultery with her in his heart' (Matthew 5:27–28). As ever, the heart of the problem lies in our heart. There is a chain reaction in our lives: thoughts become words; words become actions; actions become habits; and habits shape our character.

We are all prone to temptation. That's a fact. But it's how we deal with it that counts. Jesus went on to say, 'If your right eye causes you to sin, gouge it out and throw it away' (verse 29). For it's better to do that than to risk our ultimate destruction.

God's initiative

In his book *Money, Sex and Power*, Richard Foster explains that 'Because of sin, our sexual appetites have been distorted.' He goes on:

> The temptations are great in our sex-soaked culture. The distortions of our sexuality into lust can take a very tangled, twisted, route. Only by the grace of God and the loving support of the Christian fellowship can our lust-inflamed sexuality be straightened upright again.[5]

God's grace has already been demonstrated by the sacrifice of Jesus on the cross, where he defeated the powers that so grip us. God has taken the initiative in rescuing us from the slavery that we can fall back into and has acted to bring us back into a relationship with himself, through his Son Jesus

Christ. He has opened the door to freedom from the grip of sin in our lives through his forgiveness. The Holy Spirit is at work in our hearts to *move* us, so that we no longer find this commandment a burden, but rather a promise for our lives.

Responding to God

Whatever our workplace context we can all make a difference, even in the smallest way, for what we do at work affects not just our own lives but other people's too. What we do at work sets the tone for what we do at home and with our friends. If we can form right relationships in the workplace, we can affirm and value marriage and it will ripple through the other areas of our lives. Our work culture is invading our lives outside of work and the wave needs arresting if marriage is to be helped back into health. We need to act, for the tide is against us.

Here are some ways in which we can reinforce and support healthy relationships:

1. Keep a clean mind

How we think and what we think about are at the heart of this issue. The Bible says, 'Whatever is true, whatever is noble, whatever is right, whatever is pure, whatever is lovely, whatever is admirable – if anything is excellent or praiseworthy – think about such things' (Philippians 4:8).

We need to *want* to have a clean mind. We need to want to value marriage and right relationships. This is an act of will. The battle for marriage and for right relationships in society starts in our hearts and minds, for when the issue is settled in our hearts, it will affect what we say and do, and how we act at work in valuing marriage and healthy relationships.

2. Actively respond

Jesus says, 'If your right eye causes you to sin, gouge it out . . . ' Prompt, immediate and, if necessary, radical action is required. If we are involved in any way in a wrong relationship, we should decide to put a stop to it right now – not tomorrow, not at some point in the future when we have sorted it out, but right now. No situation is too deep or unresolved that it cannot be stopped.

If the problem is pornography, as it is for many men, let us get rid of it – today. Misuse of the internet through accessing pornography is on the increase. The high-profile resignation of the Bank of Ireland's Chief Executive occurred after a routine sweep found that he had breached company rules. In one eighteen-month period BT sacked 200 staff for downloading pornography from work computers.

We can't stop being bombarded by such images but, as J.John puts it, it is better to shun the bate than struggle on the hook. This is practical advice about a common and serious threat to many, men in particular.

Here is what Tim Chester writes about the potential for change in our lives: 'We are changed when we look at Jesus, delight in Jesus, commune with Jesus. But no-one can embrace Jesus if they are guilty of sin. So change comes only when we come "under grace" with its message of divine pardon and welcome.'[6]

3. Practise affirmation

We need to affirm marriage and right relationships in our workplace and when we are doing business, whether we are single or married. We might be able to say something at just the right time to help avoid putting someone else in a risky situation, for example. But how we do it is crucial.

It also helps to encourage positive work practices – for both ourselves and our colleagues – and avoid workplace threats to marriage (or to the marriages of those they work with or do business with).

It is good to be open about everyone's marital status. As a manager I find it is helpful to encourage married colleagues to go home at the end of the working day, rather than expect them always to have to socialize. As a manager or as an organization, we can affirm marriage in the language we use (retain the words 'wives' and 'husbands', for example), in the HR policies we adopt, such as flexible hours, childcare and equal pay, and in the social life of the workplace. In one firm where I was a partner the office Christmas party had become familiarly known as the 'grope in the garage'. I voted to stop it.

4. Take evasive action

We must act immediately when we find ourselves in a compromising situation. This can be difficult and sometimes even costly. When we are invited to a club after work or on a business trip, we need to decide before the situation arises what we are going to do. The most effective course of action when faced with a compromising situation or one that is looming is to walk away from it, or sometimes to run!

We cannot afford to work out the merits and demerits of a course of action when we are in the midst of it! As parents we told our teenagers to decide beforehand what to do when they find themselves alone on a sofa with an attractive boy/girl. Once you are there it's too late to try to work it out!

Some of us might find it helpful to adopt a few guidelines in being wise about how we spend time with the opposite sex. These might include:

- avoid business trips alone with a colleague of the opposite sex;
- avoid lunches alone together and include others where possible;
- avoid drinks or social events after work alone;
- avoid settings that will draw you together;
- avoid sharing personal feelings in ways that might develop intimacy;
- meet with others, or in the open.

5. Be selective in confrontation

The sheer power of sex and its impact on the workplace may sometimes demand confrontation. We need to be honest.

But we also need to be very cautious and wise in confronting other people's actions, lest we be seen to be interfering, or worse still, judgmental. We can easily come across as holier-than-thou or even preachy. Let's recall how Jesus dealt with the woman caught in adultery – with compassion and love.

So if an affair at work does need to be brought out in the open, it should be done lovingly and appropriately, not judgmentally. When I had to deal with such a situation, I was keen to deal with the impact on the office without in any way judging the manager involved.

6. Be accountable

When we confront sexual sin in our lives, we bring it into the light and before God, which is the best way to deal with it. An effective way to do this is to become accountable to another individual. We can do this by praying with one or more Christians in a confidential setting, allowing openness and honesty, and an opportunity to pray for healing and restoration.

Because of the sheer addictive power of internet pornography, one of the most effective means of dealing with it is through accountability, rather than simply by trying to build higher and higher barriers to the source. Software packages are available that work by sending an email to the person to whom you are accountable. A senior man once requested to be accountable to me for anything he downloaded; he never looked at a site after that, as he was simply too embarrassed that I might know.

7. Seek good maintenance

Today few of us come into marriage with much, or indeed any, practical training. We just get on with it. But we are not allowed to get into a car and drive off without passing a test on practice and theory. Such an omission is far from ideal, as even the best marriages can benefit from the essential tools and techniques that make for good foundations and maintenance.

Marriage preparation courses are increasingly available in churches and are very valuable for refreshing and investing in marriage. Nicky and Sila Lee, who developed The Marriage Course, highlight two of the greatest tools for healthy marriages:

1. The first is what they describe as 'marriage time': a kind of date-night each week, doing fun things just as a couple. It helps to keep communication open and romance alive. If the same effort and imagination devoted to affairs was given to such times, many people like Susan Greenhill would probably still be married.
2. A second foundational tool for every marriage is discovering each other's needs. Marriages thrive when we recognize and seek to meet each other's emotional

needs. But we have to discover what our partner's needs are first! Typically we give love in the way we want to receive it. So if you value time together, you will tend to give time to your spouse, even if he or she needs a different approach, such as loving actions or affirming words. We need to discern what makes our spouse feel most loved, and meeting those needs is a great discovery, as my wife Jackie and I can certainly confirm.

A marriage needs to be constantly nurtured in order to grow. We have never 'arrived'. Those who are married need to keep their relationships refreshed by investing in them continually, daily, weekly, annually, and to know that God has this vital boundary in place so that all the blessings of marriage can be enjoyed.

For reflection

1. How might you affirm the value of marriage and healthy relationships in your workplace?
2. Would people in your workplace find you able to talk about cohabitation or homosexuality non-judgmentally?
3. How might you confront an unsupportive negative practice at work in relation to marriage?
4. If you are single, are there ways in which you could develop a greater holiness at work in relation to this issue?
5. If you are married, how could you keep your marriage in better running order?

5. KEEPING THE PEACE

You shall not murder.
(Exodus 20:13)

The sixth commandment ups the stakes, as it concerns life and death.

Of all the commandments to break, this one has a finality; once done, it cannot be undone. But this sixth commandment is more than God just being against murder. It is about his affirmation of life itself and the unique value of each one of us. Most clearly of all the commandments, it sets out healthy limits on our actions, for our protection.

The news of murder and killings fills our screens and newspapers: children murdering other children, serial killers, school massacres, genocides, holocaust victims and ethnic cleansing.

Murder is the intentional taking of another's life and it involves a callous disregard for human life. The Bible teaches that life is sacred, and there are three main reasons:

First, God made us, so our life is not our own. Only God can give it and take it away. Secondly, we are made in the image of God (Genesis 1:26). Each of us, whatever our status, mental health, race, class or income, is special; we are different from the animals. Thirdly, we have a responsibility to one another. One of God's earliest instructions to us is: 'And from each man, too, I will demand an accounting for the life of his fellow man' (Genesis 9:5). We are part of a wider community, as this poem by John Donne bears out:

No man is an island entire of itself;
every man is a piece of the continent,

a part of the main . . .
Any man's death diminishes me,
because I am involved in mankind.
And therefore never send to know
for whom the bell tolls; it tolls for thee.

Murder is a big subject, and it involves controversial, current issues such as a Just War, abortion and euthanasia, which I am not qualified to tackle. My primary concern here is to relate this commandment to our working lives.

A biblical perspective

This command is given by God to his covenant community, not just to guard other people's lives, but also to protect the quality of people's relationship with God himself. John Durham puts it like this: 'What Israel faces for breaking the commandments . . . is not the loss of life, but the far worse loss of Yahweh's Presence.'[1]

Jesus takes this commandment back to its roots when he says, 'You have heard that it was said to the people long ago, "Do not murder, and anyone who murders will be subject to judgment." But I tell you that anyone who is angry with his brother will be subject to judgment' (Matthew 5:21–22a). Jesus points out that it is not just actions that lead to death; this commandment is also about what is going on in our hearts.

We only have to look at the first deadly conflict recorded in the Bible – between two brothers – to understand the connection between heart and action. Cain, the older brother, was a farmer, and Abel was a shepherd. Abel was more generous in what he brought before God. This pleased God but got up Cain's nose. He got angry about it, and so God said to him, 'Why is your face downcast? If you do what is right, will you not be accepted? But if you do not do what is right, sin is crouching at your door; it desires to have you, but you must master it' (Genesis 4:6–7).

Here God offers the *possibility* of change and points out the *danger* of not doing anything about it. Cain's anger led him to kill his own brother and, when challenged, he replied with this famous quotation: 'Am I my brother's keeper?' (Genesis 4:9). He meant it rhetorically! We see in this short story the typical human reaction: he ignores the caution, tries to sort out the problem in his own way, pretends ignorance and denies any responsibility. It looks all too familiar. We see the same cycles of behaviour at work and it starts with anger.

Anger in the workplace

There is no shortage of anger or rage in our society. Violence is being pumped into our culture through TV, books, advertising, cinema and video games. The term 'road rage' entered the dictionary in 1997. All this seeps into work life too. We will all be aware of abusive language, aggressive behaviour, sexism, ageism, racism and bullying. In some workplaces we may encounter people who seem to be full of deadly venom. Our words hurt; our looks can kill; in our thoughts we wish someone dead. All this has the stench of death about it.

Our feelings run into words, and our words into actions. I am surprised at how often aggressive attitudes are lauded in many work cultures. Individuals are promoted because of their aggressive attitude to doing deals (this was certainly the case in my old firm). Decisions can be based on retaliation for past hurts or a humiliation leading to revenge. We use opportunities to cut out a rival, because we are angry with them. We humiliate a subordinate who made a bad mistake which made us angry. Losing a deal to a competitor can spark off angry reactions to colleagues who are behaving quite normally. The printer fails at the worst moment and we fly off the handle, or some information arrives late so we shout at the assistant.

The anger expressed daily in our workplaces is rarely commented on; we just seem to take it for granted. We tolerate aggressive individuals because they are productive. Worse still, we bring our work culture home with us, as we berate our family members for poor performance or missed deadlines!

How can we tell if we have gone too far without an objective standard to measure against? That is part of the point of this commandment; what are 'acceptable' limits?

Anger at work can arise from various sources and personality types. J.John caricatures four different types of colleague:

1. **The rhino**: he or she charges at you, or just yells; they let it all spill out – over you and anyone else. They may have regrets but a temper is one thing you cannot get rid of by losing it. People who fly into a rage always make a bad landing.
2. **The mute**: these clam up. You can see the veins in their neck swell, but they are working hard to conceal it; you can hear them breathe in. They repress their anger. They swallow the pain but it eats them up. And the anger surfaces another time, in another situation.
3. **The manipulator**: this person hits back. But not like a rhino; there are no fireworks. No. This one goes for gibes, underhand or sarcastic remarks, put-downs. Often in front of others. The resentment spills out, but it remains.
4. **The martyr**: it's their fault; they are to blame. They are a doormat and invite people to walk over them.[2]

None of these is a good model of anger management! There should be a better way. God knows that we get angry. He knows our frailties and how we are vulnerable when we express anger and also when we are on the receiving end. But he wants to protect us and protect our relationship with him and with others. If we know we have a serious problem with anger, we will need professional advice. But for most of us it will help to understand where our anger comes from. Here are three possible sources:

1. Conflict

Wherever there are people, conflict is inevitable! We all have different expectations, attitudes, styles and gifts. And we are, as the Bible makes clear, naturally selfish. When we are threatened we can attack or withdraw. But unresolved conflict often leads to resentment and anger. In fact it is worth noting that 70% of workers leave their boss, not their job.

We can only change *our* end of any exchange. Tim Chester points out: 'It seems our first instinct when we want to change is to do something. We think activity will change us. We want a list of do's and don'ts.' He adds later: 'But only God can bring true and lasting change. And that's because only God can change our hearts.'[3]

We can also be complicit by our lack of action, for example, if we stand by and do nothing when a colleague is being savaged by another colleague or a manager. We fail too by being passive onlookers.

We can bring peace at work if we use mediation techniques. I am well aware of the power of mediation in resolving conflict and I have been involved in a number of workplace mediations, most with very successful outcomes.[4]

2. Stress

At the lighter end of the scale, I read that the top reason for office stress cited by graduates in the workplace was not being able to change a printer cartridge (74%). If only that were our greatest problem!

Note the following statistics:

- Bullying at work now accounts for 50% of stress-related absences (Institute of Personnel Development).
- Stress is now implicated in seven out of the top-ten killers in the world (World Health Organization).
- The Japanese have a term to describe the fate of workers who die suddenly after putting in extremely long hours – *karoshi* or 'death from overwork'. Note also the new Japanese word, *karojisatsu*, which means 'suicide from overwork' (*Associated Press*).
- The number of days taken off due to stress increased from 6.5 million to 13.5 million in the five years to 2001 (*The Guardian*).

So stress is a major cause of anger and as the pressure to perform and deliver increases, the risk of anger increases too. Sales and delivery targets, production quotas, curriculum targets, assignment deadlines, performance criteria and government-imposed targets are all regular contributory factors.

3. Fear

Fear is one of the two great motivators of the marketplace (the other being greed): fear of losing out, of losing one's job or reputation, or of being found out when you're late with a report or some information. There are so many fears out there. And when we feel threatened we become angry and attack.

Fear of failure has afflicted many workers during the recent economic downturn. There have been some well-publicized 'credit-crunch suicides' as senior people have failed to cope with an acute change in status and wealth and could no longer keep up with their peers.

Fear is one of the main root causes of anger. But the Bible says, 'There is no fear in love. But perfect love drives out fear' (1 John 4:18).

Right anger?

However, it is important to realize that there is a legitimate anger. Most of the references to anger in the Bible concern God himself. He gets angry with our attitudes and our behaviour. When Jesus found that the people – ostensibly religious people at that – were using the temple as a market-place, he was justifiably angry. So the Bible does not deny the use of anger; it teaches us how to deal with it and how to express it in an appropriate, non-destructive way.

Love in action

Without turning from grace to law, I want to suggest six ways in which we might want to cooperate with God and demon-strate his love, and so push back the boundaries of anger:

1. Practise restraint

The book of Proverbs says: 'He who answers before listening – that is his folly and his shame' (18:13). Similarly, Jesus' brother James says, 'Everyone should be quick to listen, slow to speak and slow to become angry' (James 1:19). It is all too easy to react by saying the wrong thing. So we are urged to listen, and then come back later to tackle the issue after the heat has passed and we can choose our words carefully. It's not weakness, even if the office culture is combative. Meekness is not weakness, and peace of mind is better than giving someone else a piece of *our* mind.

We are not to brush issues under the carpet, nor are we to be doormats; we are to deal with them. It is OK to feel angry when we have been badly treated, unfairly criticized or poorly managed.

As God said to Cain: 'If you do what is right, will you not be accepted?' (Genesis 4:7). Often, coming back and doing or saying the right thing can lead to acceptance by the other person. The liberating truth for Christians is that it is not *our place* to avenge a situation when we have been treated unjustly. Ultimately we are to leave it with God, because he will put it right in eternity. Paul writes: 'Do not repay anyone evil for evil' (Romans 12:17), and 'Do not take revenge, my friends, but leave room for God's wrath, for it is written: "It is mine to avenge; I will repay," says the Lord' (verse 19).

2. Express appreciation

In a critical environment, people say such things as: 'I've been saying this for years but he never listens' or 'It's typical of her!' A powerful way to avoid conflict and the anger that can follow is to express appreciation. We can best do this routinely as a matter of habit. It's wise to preface what we feed back to others with a positive statement, for when we speak appreciatively of others it disarms the critic.

As we recognize our differences of temperament, personality and background, we can gain a greater understanding of the other person. After all, who am I to judge someone else? As Jesus put it: 'Why do you look at the speck of sawdust in your brother's eye and pay no attention to the plank in your own eye?' (Matthew 7:3).

We don't seek to change the other person – rather to complement them: to look for one another's strengths and support one another's weaknesses. Romans 15:7 says, 'Accept one another, then, just as Christ accepted you . . . ' As Christians we may want to pray for the person who is causing us problems. But mainly we are to pray for change in our own heart, for God to change *our* attitude. This will diffuse angry thoughts.

3. Try negotiation

The best way to resolve conflict in the workplace is to negotiate a solution, rather than through counter-attack or surrender. Here are six steps to peace:

1. Find a good time and place to meet.
2. Identify the issue.
3. Discuss the issue, rather than personalize it (avoid 'You always . . . ' or 'You never . . . '). You may want to use a visual aid to represent the issue to keep it neutral and 'out there'.
4. Work out the possible options together.
5. Decide on the best course of action.
6. Be prepared to re-evaluate.

In some cases you may find it appropriate to use a mediator who can help the parties to communicate in a controlled way and find a resolution to their conflict. In the Sermon on the Mount Jesus said to his followers, 'Blessed are the peacemakers, for they will be called sons of God' (Matthew 5:9). That verse inspired me to develop my role as a mediator.

4. Forgive quickly

If you have been angry with someone, go to them, apologize and be reconciled. Forgiveness is the key remedy. As Jesus taught in the Lord's Prayer: 'Forgive us our debts, as we *also* have forgiven our debtors' (Matthew 6:12, emphasis added). We can take the initiative and experience the liberation.

In either scenario – whether we are being forgiven or forgiving someone else – we have to face the reality of what was done or said. I need to admit it to myself, to the other person and to God. Before we can defeat anger we must first stop deceiving ourselves. If we don't face it and talk it through, sooner or later we will take it out on someone else.

Channel 4's *The New Ten Commandments* ended with a powerful workplace story about the power of forgiveness:

> Stephen Korsa-Acqua was just eighteen when he graduated to armed robbery. His gang operated nationwide, hitting banks, security vans and building societies. On 6 April 1983, Stephen had just stolen £35,000 from a Bristol bank and was looking for a getaway car when he ran into police constable Billy Burns.
>
> Billy was unarmed. Stephen shot him through the face. Billy survived, saved by his teeth, which slowed the bullet. Stephen was captured and sent down for twenty-five years.
>
> The following year, Billy and his wife sent Stephen a Christmas card in prison. He and his family are Christians and felt that they would become bitter and twisted if they couldn't forgive Stephen for what he had done.
>
> Several years after that, Stephen wrote a long letter to Billy, who eventually came to visit him in prison. Stephen was physically shaking when they met. It was the hardest thing he had ever done in his life.
>
> Billy and Stephen became friends. Today they run a project for young people called Inside Out. They explain to kids that the criminal world is not glamorous.

The power of forgiveness can be imported into every workplace, by us.

5. Go the extra mile

As he so often did in the Sermon on the Mount, Jesus confronts popular culture: 'You have heard that it was said, "Eye for eye, and tooth for tooth." But I tell you, Do not resist an evil person' (Matthew 5:38–39). He goes on to say that we should turn the other cheek, to give our cloak when our tunic is taken, to go two miles if forced to go one: 'Give to the one who asks you, and do not turn away from the one who wants to borrow from you' (verse 42).

This was radical stuff at the time, very countercultural. So what does that look like in our contemporary work culture? Perhaps your manager slates you for a late report in front of the team; you, however, graciously thank her for over-looking the previous one which was also late. Or a colleague takes your laptop into a meeting (a great inconvenience), but when he returns you offer to help him with his next PowerPoint presentation. Or perhaps your manager makes you work an extra hour, but you offer to work for two.

That can have such an impact: on God, on you and on others.

6. Cultivate the Creator's love

After his teaching on the 'extra mile' Jesus moves on immediately to urging his listeners to love their enemies: 'You have heard that it was said, "Love your neighbour and hate your enemy." But I tell you: Love your enemies and pray for those who persecute you, that you may be sons of your Father in heaven' (Matthew 5:43–45).

Jesus points out that it's easy to love those who love us. But it's so difficult to act lovingly to our colleagues who don't. It's also hard to love others when we don't love ourselves. We feel defensive and are easily wounded. We hit back when we are hurt. But God is love and we all need to experience his love, to know in our hearts that he loves us. Even at work? Especially at work!

When we know God's love, we are in a stronger position to take anger and not to give it.

For reflection

1. What makes you angry at work?
2. How do you respond to other people's anger at work?
3. How might you be able to act differently?

6. LIVING WITH OUR PAST

Honour your father and your mother,
so that you may live long in the land
the LORD your God is giving you.
(Exodus 20:12)

The focus of the fifth commandment is on the health of family life: 'Just as the relationship with Yahweh is the beginning of the covenant, so this relationship is the beginning of society, the inevitable point of departure for every human relationship.'[1] And it still applies to us as adults, even though the outworking of it is different in the workplace. We honour our parents (or parents-in-law) at work by the positive way we refer to them or talk about them. For some of us we may not have much that is positive to say, but we can usually find something.

This commandment also speaks to us about the respect due to older people within the workplace, and their valuable role as mentors to younger workers. It challenges ageism in our work culture. With the changes to retirement ages and increasingly longer working lives, this is now a live issue.

I also believe that our own experience of being parented profoundly affects us and continues to do so into adulthood, including influencing how we behave at work. Our view of our own parents – positive and negative – can affect our view of those in authority over us at work and how we value older colleagues.

And for workers who become parents themselves, it is important to teach them the values that lie at the heart of this commandment too.

The value of parental role models

Positive father or mother figures can be a huge encouragement to our development, and we often find them at work.
I am thinking of people who are prepared to give advice and
make positive suggestions, but who can also give constructive
criticism. It might be a foreman or a manager who takes an
interest, listens to us and encourages us. I have often seen the
value that such figures represent to younger colleagues, as
they take time out to further an individual's career or develop
their skills.

I was struck again by this recently when I was reviewing
progress on projects with two junior colleagues. In both cases,
other issues came up and I realized they needed some encouragement, remembering that their relationship with their own
fathers was not as positive as they perhaps needed. I had
another role to fulfil!

Many years ago, when I started a new department within
a large property advisory firm, I was young, inexperienced
and had never worked in a consultancy context, as I had come
straight from a period in local government. After I had helped
the senior partner in a major department with one of his deals,
he took me under his wing and then championed my career
in the firm. We need to honour such people, especially as
we in turn grow and they perhaps become less influential.
Younger workers have to make the tricky transition from
college to work – where suddenly they're no longer mixing
solely with their own generation, but with lots of older people.

Dead meat at fifty-five?

A friend of mine who had worked for many years in the
banking sector was made redundant twice in five years. He
turned to look outside the City, not because he couldn't get a
job, but because he didn't believe he could survive another

redundancy and *then* get another job. 'At fifty-five you are dead meat,' he said. Our work culture is increasingly ageist. Despite the government urging us to work longer, our organizations still favour younger people. We can each play our part in pushing back by, for example, encouraging and supporting HR polices that allow older people to remain active in work.

We need to acknowledge the wisdom and experience of older people at work and encourage them to take on the role of mentors to younger workers. We should treat them with respect, and encourage and support ways of keeping them productive and useful if they are able, for the good of the organization and their own self-esteem.

Tony Campolo comments: 'For some [retirement] may be a welcome period of life, but for most people it is covertly dreaded.'[2] He describes how we regard the retired and elderly as 'throwaway people', those who are no longer of any economic value, discarded and eventually to be hidden away in some care home. Surely what many need is not a complete halt to productive work, but a career change or a progressive reduction in workload. When I was a partner in a large property firm, the practice's doctor was very critical of a policy that required partners to work full tilt to the age of sixty and then retire. He considered it to be unhealthy. Indeed, some did not live very long after retirement.

Ageism does not honour older workers. So how we can combat it? We can encourage our employers (or partners or directors, if we are in leadership) to adopt much more flexible HR polices that suit the needs of older workers, for example, a gradual reduction in workload and/or responsibilities, matched by a proportionate reduction in rewards. The process could also involve a progressive passing on of skills (or clients or contacts) so that the organization and the individuals within it could continue to benefit from the workers' wisdom, experience and other valuable contributions to the business over the years.

We also honour older people at work by how we treat them personally and directly. We need to consider how we show them that we value and respect them by how we interact with them. I confess, I have not always done that well.

The effects of our parenting

Some of the most confident and independent (in a good way) fellow-workers I know have, I've discovered, been the product of a happy marriage and a healthy home. Many people are fortunate enough to have gained enormously from their upbringing and feel that in their working life they 'stand on the shoulders of giants'. Where this is the case, we honour those giants – our parents – by acknowledging their positive influence on us.

But more and more I am becoming aware of how people's childhood relationship with their parents has adversely influenced them at work, even when they are well into their middle age. For example, I came across an investment banker who has developed elaborate strategies to avoid certain social settings because his mother abandoned him as a child. I know a former futures trader who managed to get through the day only by using cocaine in order to deaden the pain of his abuse as a child. An architect I know is so driven to succeed because his parents only gave him conditional love.

Philip Larkin famously expressed the impact of poor parenting in his poem, 'This Be the Verse'.[3] The opening stanza has an expletive which has made it memorable; but leaving that aside, what the poet is getting across is the message that while our parents don't necessarily mean to mess us up, they all too often do, sometimes leaving us with the legacy of their own faults as well – as if thrown in for good measure! This proposition has the echo of the biblical principle that the sins of the father will be visited to the third and fourth generations. What we do as parents has an impact on our children and their children's children, spiritually.

God as Father

The way we were parented, particularly by our father, can affect our view of God as Father. But the Bible portrays God the Father as everything a parent should be. It's not that we look at a good dad and say that is what God the Father is like. It's the other way around: the Bible gives us a picture of a perfect father, of a God who listens, understands, keeps his promises, is always there, disciplines us with love (for that is loving) and loves us unconditionally. So the best way we can honour our natural or adoptive / foster parents is to know God as Father. In him we can be secure as we face our past.

We may have unresolved resentments towards our parents, or our parenting experience may mean that we are still carrying around our baggage: we take it to work every day and it is affecting us and others. And we find that it's not getting any lighter. For some the trauma of their own parenting means they may well need professional help. But for most of us, we will just need to face up to it and deal with it.

For some it may require an act of will to forgive a parent or to seek forgiveness. For others, it may be an action – writing a letter perhaps. Many of us need to be better equipped as parents ourselves, to find ways of doing things differently. In my case my parents were hopeless at resolving conflict. Everything was tucked under the carpet! So I found myself doing the same; and I still have a tendency to avoid conflict. I had no model of how to cope with it. It was my wife who helped me to see that dealing with conflict, though difficult, is the better way. In our own marriage situations she modelled to me ways of getting issues out in the open to resolve them, without it being too personal. Rather than avoiding conflict, I am now more inclined to put into practice what I have learned from her, from The Marriage Course, and from my training as a mediator. But it has taken time.

Giving honour; receiving the promise

Even if we have very negative feelings towards our parents, this commandment still demands that we honour them. Isn't that too difficult? Actually it's the secret to our freedom, because how we behave towards them also affects us. As we honour our parents, we let go of any ill-feeling and lessen the hold of any bitterness, removing the bonds that may tie us down. If they are still alive, we honour them in the way we address them, in the way we speak about them to others and in the way we prefer their needs to our own.

What does this mean in relation to the workplace? While we don't want to be unrealistic about our parents, we can always speak well of them as best we can. So when the subject of parents comes up – which it can often do with negative undertones – we can choose not to join in. We can move away or move the conversation on. Or we can actively chip in a contribution that gives honour to our parents by being positive without sounding self-righteous. In doing so it may change the tone of that particular conversation or even the way workmates talk about their own parents when you are around. I am pleasantly surprised by how often this happens.

This is the only commandment that comes with a promise: ' . . . so that you may live long in the land'. We give and so we receive. I understand this promise to mean that we are better able to enjoy the fruit of the kingdom ('the land' in Old Testament terminology). By giving honour to our parents we are more whole.

But there is another dimension: God moves in our hearts to give honour, not out of duty or obligation, but out of love, in response to what he has done for each of us. The commandment itself becomes a promise. We will *want* to honour our mother and father.

Honouring *all* fathers and mothers

God affirms families and the relationships within them. He is concerned to protect family life. There are biblical standards and guidelines for parental care, discipline and the welfare of the whole family. But the Bible is quite realistic about the difficulties of achieving good, healthy, family relationships. Indeed, many of the great figures, such as Abraham, Isaac or David, had dysfunctional families! Neglectful or abusive families can cause great harm, but this does not make families redundant. Families remain the biblical model, where children are raised by their parents in a secure, loving, lifelong relationship.

Growing up in a happy and healthy family can be an amazing experience. It provides a loving, secure environment where we can grow in confidence and learn how to relate to one another and how to resolve conflicts; it is where we learn our values, how to communicate and become self-controlled, confident adults. It's where we are loved unconditionally and whence we go out into the world, equipped to be independent and adult.

Homestead
Home is our sacred shelter
in the storm.
The leeward side.
Our high tower –
gathering its lords
back to itself.

A haven:
Safeguarding her own.
The place of healing –
of our inmost fears.
Our refuge within
its enclosure.
Where we go out from –
to meet the world.[4]

I was fortunate enough to have been brought up in a stable family, though my parents did not have what I would describe as a happy marriage. I have since been blessed with a very happy marriage, which has produced four wonderful children, who are themselves all now married and parenting children of their own.

Family life is changing. It is very different from what it was fifty years ago. Then one could know exactly who everyone was and how they related to one another. Roles were clearly defined and fixed. Today the word 'family' denotes an altogether more fluid and fragmented arrangement, sometimes referring to a group who may not all live under the same roof or have the same mother and father. Nor will family groups necessarily stay the same over their lifetime. Although this presents challenges, many good things have come out of the changes in family life, such as an increase in shared parental responsibility, greater value given to women and the freedom to escape from abusive family set-ups.

But not all is well with the family in the UK: divorce affects a quarter of all children by the age of sixteen; 40% of children are now born outside of marriage; over 25% of people now live alone (partly because of family breakdown). This affects us as individuals, as well as society at large, in many areas of our lives, such as our physical well-being, mental health, ability to relate to others, behaviour, insecurities and poor self-esteem.

Good families make for a healthy society. The Landmark Report for The Children's Society, 'A Good Childhood', published some stark conclusions. *The Sunday Times* reported that: 'Britain's cult of individualism, greed and selfishness has so blighted children's lives that families and pupils need basic training in love and moral responsibility . . . One of the most controversial areas covered by the report is the effect of women working.'[5] Feckless fathers also came in for criticism. As parents we are not spending enough time with our children. The report also recommended improvements to the way leave entitlements are administered.

However, parenting is not just an issue for married people or those who aspire to marriage. It affects us all. One of the greatest and subtlest threats to society is a growing underclass in the UK – believed to be approaching 20% of the population: in official parlance they are NEETs – people Not in Employment, Education or Training. The key indicator of this significant group, whose lives are at a significantly higher risk of poor health, crime and benefit dependence, is births to unmarried mothers. The crisis is not so much about single mothers as absent fathers. This is a controversial but important area of debate.

Work and family life
Our work culture is one of the greatest causes of pressure on parents, and we all contribute to this pressure.

First, we spend too many hours working. A target of 2,000 billable hours a year is not uncommon among large professional and consulting firms in central London. In a recent major survey of our time, 36% of women thought they could achieve just as much work in fewer hours, while

23% of professionals with children take work home once a week.

Secondly, work is stressful: absences due to stress are on the increase. For some of us, our minds are so full when we get home that we are absent even when we are there. Rob Parsons, a family life counsellor and successful lawyer, tells of the time when he was very busy and was mentally somewhere else even when he got home. His daughter got up on a chair and shouted in his ear, 'Is there anyone in there?!'

I remember with great affection a client of mine called George Best (not the footballer!), who was Managing Director of a Yorkshire-based property company. At the end of a long all-day meeting in Leeds he would usher me into his office and fetch a toy or a model kit from his cupboard. Thrusting it into my hands, he would say, 'Don't do what I did – spend time with your family.' I had small children at the time and it helped me to resolve to put boundaries around my time.

Commenting on a survey about the use of time, Sir Larry Robinson, a company chairman, recently said, 'The most important thing I've learned in business is that most things you do aren't necessary.' He concluded: 'In my view, the only time really worth spending is time with the family. That's when you should be as loose as it needs to be. There should be no pressure.'

The Archbishop of Canterbury, Dr Rowan Williams, spoke out on childhood and parenting a few years ago when he called on us all to grow up and accused our 'culture of work' of contributing to the neglect of the family by ignoring the requirements for creating stable and secure environments.

In an increasingly fragmented society, those who are parents in stable and secure environments are likely to be in the minority. They need help. We need to support family-friendly work practices where they are viable.

Loving responses

How might we respond to God's initiative and keep this commandment in our workplaces?

1. Show respect

The Bible is full of wisdom on this subject: for example, 'Listen to your father, who gave you life, and do not despise your mother when she is old' (Proverbs 23:22). We can show respect to our parents when we support them in old age and when we share our own children with them: 'Children's children are a crown to the aged, and parents are the pride of their children' (Proverbs 17:6).

We can respect older people at work by appreciating their contribution, especially their wisdom and the value of their experience to those who are at much earlier stages of their career.

2. Affirm parenting

Parents are doing a very difficult job at home and we can help them – usually by small acts of kindness or support. For example, we can encourage young mothers and fathers to go home at the end of the day, rather than 'meet you at the bar' – sometimes we need saving from ourselves.

As an employer I support flexible work practices. One of my senior planners was able to work three days a week so that she could care for her son. Two of the most senior professionals in the office each work four days, in order to take over childcare from their wives and allow them time out.

3. Choose acceptance

We need to accept our parents as they really are. The Bible is not asking us to look back with rose-tinted glasses. We have to be realistic, even if we don't like what we see. We are not being asked to like them or even to accept any wrong behaviours or values just because they are our parents. We are to honour our parents as human beings and accept them as people, despite their faults and failings.

4. Offer appreciation

Whatever our experience, we can usually find something to thank our parents for – even if it is just for the effort of bringing us up. Parenting is one of the most difficult jobs anyone can take on, and I speak from experience, with four children of my own (though my wife can certainly take most of the credit)! Individual circumstances can make it much harder, for example, parenting alone, lack of money, or ill-health. We can also appreciate our parents for what we have learned; we will often have picked up from them more than we realize. We can acknowledge what the Bible calls their wisdom. The book of Proverbs contains many wise instructions from a parent to an offspring: for example, 'My son, keep your father's commands and do not forsake your mother's teaching' (Proverbs 6:20).

The best way to express our appreciation is obviously to our parents directly: in the way we ask or listen, in seeking their advice or opinion, by being considerate and mindful of their needs. And we can continue to honour them after their death (not that we should wait till then!).

A friend of mine who worked in the City had a difficult relationship with his mother, especially when she became old, infirm and very critical in spirit. I think he came to accept her but he struggled to find a way of expressing any appreciation for her, especially at her death. He read this at her funeral:

Gone
She is gone
And I will grieve
For a time.

Then I will recall
How she was
When we were young.

I will dismiss
The recent memories
Of her latter years.

I will rejoice
In all she gave
When I could receive.

Then I will give thanks
For who she was
And what she made me.[6]

In those words he found a way of accepting her for who she was; he was honest but was able to honour her by expressing his acceptance and appreciation publicly.

5. Establish boundaries
If you are feeling the pressure of balancing work and parenting, you will need to establish boundaries. Unless a priority in favour of home can be established and enforced, the pressures will almost always come from work. This is certainly true of the lawyers and bankers in the City, where the work culture is dominated by long hours.

Establishing boundaries is not easy, and it has to start with a desire in our heart and a recognition that it is necessary. Both parents need to be in agreement and recognize the implications. Most of us will have to negotiate such boundaries with our manager (and often colleagues) at our workplace.

Securing your boundaries could affect promotion or even long-term career prospects in a particular firm or organization. But it is worth it. I have no doubt that I could have been more overtly 'successful' if I had been prepared to sacrifice more family time. But when our children were smaller, I resolved to limit my working day to ten hours and not take work home (especially at weekends).

Sometimes it can be the other way around, with family pressures intruding on work and the danger that the worker becomes unable to fulfil his or her obligations properly to employer or colleagues. This needs addressing too.

6. Agree clear expectations

This is where we can so often fall down. It is vital to reconcile the expectations of both home and work. For example, it would be simply disastrous to arrange with your spouse to be home by 6.30 without agreeing such an expectation with your manager who may want you to work late. Be up front with both and explain the problem so that you can meet their expectations without conflict (especially inner conflict).

I believe this is particularly important for fathers of sons. Susan Faludi, a social commentator who spent six years working on a book about masculinity published at the start of the twenty-first century, wrote this:

> From the start, I intended to talk to the young men about
> such matters as work, sport, marriage, religion, war and
> entertainment, but what they really wanted to talk about

was their fathers . . . 'My father never taught me how to be a man' was the single line I heard again and again.[7]

Important to God

Parents are important to God: they are the foundation of family life and the successful upbringing of children. Let us do all we can in our workplace to help family life thrive.

For reflection

1. Do you manage to find ways to express honour for your parents?
2. Have you got clear boundaries in place?
3. Are you successfully managing the expectations of home and work?

7. KEEPING A BALANCE

Remember the Sabbath day by keeping it holy.
Six days you shall labour and do all your work, but the seventh
day is a Sabbath to the LORD your God. On it you shall not do
any work, neither you, nor your son or daughter, nor your
manservant or maidservant, nor your animals, nor the alien
within your gates. For in six days the LORD made the heavens
and the earth, the sea, and all that is in them,
but he rested on the seventh day. Therefore the LORD
blessed the Sabbath day and made it holy.
(Exodus 20:8–11)

The fourth commandment is the longest and the one most directly relevant to work. But it's not just about work. The Sabbath is so much more than the restful end of a weary week: it is what the week has been working towards: a day that belongs to God, one that he has poured his blessing into and one that is holy (separate). It is a day set apart from other days, when we can delight in God and his creation, rest like him, and reflect on how he has blessed us.

In the past this commandment has so often been turned into legalism, as each generation has sought to implement what it means in the public sphere. We have found it so hard to penetrate its inner meaning and value, both to God and to ourselves as his people, that we (as it seemed to others) have carved out this day to shut up joy and ban all pleasures. No wonder we have now gone the other way, so that Sunday is utterly indistinguishable from Saturday.

Norman Wirzba, in his delightful book *Living the Sabbath*, explains something of the manifold meaning in this commandment: 'This command takes us back to the founding of the created order itself, showing us that Sabbath observance is not an incidental part of life.'[1] He goes on to explore how we can discover the rhythms of rest and delight, as we live out Sabbath principles in our daily lives, applying them to work, the economy, the environment and worship.

This commandment particularly speaks to us about keeping a balanced work life and applies not just to us personally, or to our family, but corporately – to all who work. In fact it includes all the means of production to get the 'now work' message across. The commandment is echoed later in Exodus 31:12, emphasizing that it's quite serious to God, and there was a high penalty for the covenant community if it was violated.

God liberates us by his commandments: Jesus brings life. When we live and work his way we are rejuvenated, and the effects of observing Sabbath principles could ripple through the whole workforce. As a wise rabbi wrote, 'It was not Israel that kept the Sabbath, so much as the Sabbath that kept Israel.'[2]

This commandment puts limits on work, which so often dominates our time, energy and thoughts. It sets it in the context of God's work of creation and the pattern he followed – of working and pausing, delighting and then resting. These Sabbath rhythms or patterns are just as relevant today, given the frantic, stressful, over-connected, task-oriented, productivity-driven world in which most of us work. They help us to become more human and also more Christ-centred.

Holy day or holiday?

Is Sunday a holy day or a holiday? Or perhaps it should be neither. In AD 321 when Emperor Constantine declared that Sunday would henceforth be a holiday, he did not make it 'the Lord's day' (perhaps to avoid offending the myriad sun-worshippers of the time). Since then, the history of the Sabbath in Western culture has varied hugely between exponents of holy day and holiday. After the English Civil War, for example, sabbatarianism became a matter of legislation. Today, writes Stephen Miller, 'the loss of a Sabbath is . . . inescapable'.[3]

The psalmist wrote: 'This is the day the LORD has made; let us rejoice and be glad in it' (Psalm 118:24), but Mark Twain disagreed. In his satirical work, *Extracts from Adam's Diary, Translated from the Original MS.*, he recorded the following entry:

> SUNDAY – Pulled through. This day is getting to be more and more trying. It was selected and set apart last November as a day of rest. I already had six of them per week before. This is another of those unaccountable things.[4]

Later, however, he records that Adam wrote: 'I have come to like Sunday myself. Superintending tires the body so. There ought to be more Sundays. In the old days they were tough; now they come in handy.'

More recently in Channel 4's *The New Ten Commandments*, this commandment was the second one to be voted out. The celebrity Caprice commented: 'Let's be realistic.' Others remarked: 'Sunday used to be so depressing'; 'Now we have shopping 24/7'; or 'And anyway, Sunday is for football.'

Delightful or dismal?

Norman Wirzba asserts:

> The fact that Sabbath observance has a low priority for many people in our society indicates a profound confusion about what the Sabbath means. It ought to be our highest priority

and our deepest desire, because the experience of delight is what the Sabbath is all about.[5]

That the Sabbath has such a low priority is understandable. For many it is associated with dreary Sunday services and lists of prohibitions. The efforts of sabbatarians in the past, with their emphasis on legalistic adherence, have only served to reinforce this view. If the positive value of the Sabbath is missing, especially while humankind has been looking more and more to be entertained, it is hardly surprising that people have found Sundays boring.

Work and rest
We are masters of so much, but even the most powerful can't create more time. So we cram more and more activity into the time we have. Mobile phones, laptops and my BlackBerry all keep me in touch. But the lunch break is virtually history. In a recent survey of over 2,000 workers, almost 80% often work through their lunch hour, about the same percentage eat at their desks, only slightly fewer prefer email to a lunch date (rather sad!), and over 75% don't take morning or afternoon breaks.

So perhaps it's not surprising that 60% of successful professionals say they are suffering from chronic tiredness, stress or depression; over two thirds of managers are looking for a greater sense of meaning from their work; and highly skilled women are quitting their jobs as they struggle to balance work and family.

Too many people have become immersed in their work, perhaps because they have surrendered to it. For some, work is addictive. For others it can be a refuge from difficult or absent relationships. I have met many people at all levels for whom work defines who they are, as it affords them status, power, wealth and affirmation and becomes their 'domain'. Paul Valler writes frankly about his own experiences and the challenge of achieving a sensible work–life balance in his book *Get a Life*.[6] He explains how so often we are just plain tired and sometimes feel trapped in what we are doing, and so, instead of being at peace, we are troubled.

In the pursuit for more and more productive time, we are losing more than we gain. We feel guilty about relaxing; we fret when we do not have enough to do; we are constantly tired; our lives are not satisfying; and we have forgotten the purpose of work and the limitations God has placed on it. In short, we have lost our balance, like a gyroscope going off course.

So where have we gone wrong? I have much sympathy for Wirzba's diagnosis. He contends that we have moved from *being* to *having* and now to *appearing*. In the process, things have less significance and we have lost the ability to experience and appreciate the world as God's creation (in its widest sense). Instead we are fed a form of reality by marketeers, image consultants and spin doctors that robs us of our capacity to delight in, and show gratitude and praise for, the many blessings that make our life possible and a joy.

We get bored, so we fill our lives with more activity – such as work. And we crave entertainment, so we demand that our Sunday is a performance. We have become seriously out of kilter with God's purposes. But before we move on to explore those issues in relation to work, let us first consider two areas where this commandment is particularly relevant: the purpose and limitations of work.

The purpose of work

By setting out the thrust of this commandment in the context of the creation account, the Bible gives us a clue as to the *purpose* of work. It has four facets:

1. We are made for work

God is a worker

We see this in the wording of this commandment. The Bible opens with an account of God's activity of creating:

> By the seventh day God had finished the work he had been doing; so on the seventh day he rested from all his work. And God blessed the seventh day and made it holy, because on it he rested from all the work of creating that he had done.
> (Genesis 2:2–3)

And God is still working: Jesus said, 'My Father is always at his work to this very day, and I, too, am working' (John 5:17). Work is therefore part of God's character and activity.

We are created in God's image

> Then God said, 'Let us make man in our image, in our likeness, and let them rule . . . '

> So God created man
>   in his own image,
> in the image of God
>   he created him;
> male and female
>   he created them.
> (Genesis 1:26–27)

This implies that we too have the capacity and desire to work, to work well and to work creatively.

We were made for work

The Garden of Eden described in Genesis 2:4–14 was a very special place. It is significant that the heavens *and* the earth were included in God's assessment that his creation was good (verse 4). It was a place that was pleasing to the eye, good for food (verse 9) and where God walked in the cool of the day (Genesis 3:8).

In Genesis 2:15 God gives humankind purpose: 'The LORD God took the man and put him in the Garden of Eden to *work* it and take care of it' (emphasis added). If Eden needed to be worked and taken care of, how much more is this true of our modern world?! One of Adam's first tasks was naming the animals (2:19). So work is good and it matters to God. It is part of God's original plan for us and it is a primary activity for us.

2. Why work can be so difficult

We blew it. The account of the fall in Genesis 3 gives us an understanding of why the world of work can be so difficult. Three key actions stitched us up: we were fooled by the tempter, we rebelled against God and we fell out with one another (3:1–13). And we are still doing this today! God's responses nail the three main players: the devil is cursed; the woman is rebuked; and the man is sentenced to hard labour (3:14–19): 'Cursed is the ground because of you; through painful toil you will eat of it all the days of your life (verse 17); 'By the sweat of your brow you will eat your food until you return to the ground' (verse 19).

The *context* of work was cursed, not work itself. This is an important distinction. What it also tells us is that when we work for *ourselves*, leaving God out, we will be disappointed and we will never be satisfied. When we disobey God and don't trust in him – including in the context of our work – we will often hurt ourselves and possibly hurt others.

Despite the toil involved we are to work for and before God. There is a wonderful though short insight as to what this means later in the Genesis account, in the reference to Nimrod: 'Cush was the father of Nimrod, who grew to be a mighty warrior on the earth. He was a mighty hunter before the LORD; that is why it is said, "Like Nimrod, a mighty hunter before the Lord"' (Genesis 10:8–9). What is a mighty accountant 'before the Lord'? Or a mighty teacher, nurse, plumber, estate agent . . . 'before the Lord'? We could think through the implications for our own job title!

3. The New Testament makes it clear that we work for God

As Christians we have been redeemed: bought at a price. We are no longer our own but *his*. We are *in Christ*, living by faith. Now our primary *desire* is to love God and love our neighbour, not ourselves. As Christians we are different – but not odd! Our primary *motivation* is to seek first his kingdom (Matthew 6:33), knowing that 'all these things will be given to [us] as well'.

This has a huge impact on our worldview and consequently on our view of the world of work, as it frees us from the tyranny of work and we are no longer its slaves. Now we know *who* we are working for and the nature of our reward, so we no longer allow work to dictate how we spend our time. The Bible says, 'Whatever you do, work at it with all your heart, as working for the Lord, not for men, since you know that you will receive an inheritance from the Lord as a reward. It is the Lord Christ you are serving' (Colossians 3:23–24).

This is so helpful: it means we are not working *primarily* for money – not even to give away to the church or some worthy cause or to support our families. Though as a secondary aim, the Bible says we *must* earn money to support ourselves: 'If a man will not work, he shall not eat' (2 Thessalonians 3:10). Nor are we *primarily* at work to evangelize: I am not at work just to witness. In working for Christ we are liberated; if we are 'in Christ' we are strengthened and no longer alone.

4. Why the workplace matters to God

Mark Greene puts forward three primary values of work: they are instrumental, intrinsic and strategic. 'Instrumental' refers to getting things done: to provide, to educate and to finance. 'Intrinsic' means work for its own worth, to be enjoyed, to be fulfilling and because we are wired up for it (I think of the runner Eric Liddell in the film *Chariots of Fire*). 'Strategic' is about transforming the main arenas of our lives. The workplace is a primary setting for spreading the gospel of Jesus Christ. It is where many of us have most contact with others and where many of our meaningful relationships take place.

Limitations on work

Another dimension to this commandment concerns the limitations it places on work. The fourth commandment seems to be a straightforward prohibition – not to work on the Sabbath. But as we look more closely, we see that it has far greater significance. God's pattern of working was to stop at the end of each day, and reflect and delight in what he had done: 'And God saw that it was good' (see Genesis 1). But on the seventh day he rested, because he had finished his work in the previous six.

God knows that we need this pattern of reflection and resting too. He knows our frailties and our vulnerability to excessive work – what can happen to our health, our relationships, our families and so on if we just keep going without a break. And he knows our need for quality time with him.

As with all the commandments, God puts a boundary around a freedom. This day is important to God, important for us and important for everyone else (society). For example, in the survey we looked at in chapter 6 on the use of time, nearly three quarters of those interviewed spent no time at all on their own spiritual enhancement. The declaration of this commandment is that we all need to have a Sabbath – for the sake of our health, our relationships and our spirituality.

Challenges of work

It is no longer an easy thing to preserve the Sabbath as a separate day: a large number of people work shift patterns or rotas that include Sundays, and many don't get Sundays off: carers, police officers, members of the armed forces, medical staff, emergency service workers and those required to work Sundays in retail as part of their contract. Also many home-workers, mainly mothers with children, cannot take Sundays off. So it's just not possible for all of us to take off the same day. Another day, or perhaps another collection of times, will have to be found.

We shouldn't feel guilty about this, as there are many other ways of achieving the main aims of the Sabbath. It could mean dividing the equivalent of Sunday into chunks: a time of prayer with others; a time of reading Scripture (or hearing it read, perhaps on the radio or as an audio book); finding a time for the breaking of bread and fellowship with other Christians. But above all, we should arrange a collection of times that are set apart, and make them times to delight and reflect and rest, as God did in creation – times spent focusing on God and what he has done.

The communal dimension – worshipping God as a community – is obviously more achievable if we can share the same day off. Hence Christians make Sabbath worship a priority if they are able. Originally that day was Saturday, the Jewish Sabbath. After Constantine the historical pattern became established, and Sunday still remains the best day of rest.

These days Sunday is much like any other day: town centres are full, garden centres are crowded, and there is youth football everywhere. But I am not talking about turning the clocks back to the 1950s and closing everything down. Nor is this a call to shut ourselves away in a gloomy religious huddle when everyone else is enjoying themselves. We simply have to find the space for ourselves, as the space is not going to find us.

Sabbath times
There are four uses of our Sabbath 'time':

1. Rest
Sabbath enables us to take rest seriously. At one level it allows us simply to recharge our batteries, to relax and be rested physically and mentally. It breaks into our busy work cycle, allowing us to take a much-needed break.

Wilberforce, the great anti-slavery campaigner, was a tireless worker, inside and outside Parliament, but he always rested on Sundays. Later in life, reflecting on those contemporaries who had cracked under the pressure of politics, he wrote: 'With peaceful Sundays, the strings would never have snapped from over-tension!'

2. Reflection and delight
A Sabbath enables us to reflect on what we have done, which was God's pattern, and to say, 'And it was good!' I was very struck by a survey of octogenarians, who were asked, in looking back over their lives, what they would have done differently. Two consistent themes came through: they would have *risked* more and *reflected* more.

Norman Wirzba would add that in our Sabbath observance we should also practise delight.

3. Time that dethrones the rule of work

Our lives have more value than just working. A Sabbath helps us to be defined by who we are, rather than by what we do; it is an antidote to workaholism and overwork. We are reminded that we are not slaves to our work, because free people can choose not to work; slaves can't. A Sabbath reminds us of our humanity – that we ourselves have limitations and none of us is indispensable, though we love to be busy and / or the centre of things. It helps confront fear – too many of us work long hours or take our work home, because we are fearful of losing our jobs or we worry about the need to keep up. But as Christians, we are to trust God – even with our work.

Is work becoming our God? By keeping God's day of rest we proclaim that *God* is Lord of our time and our lives. He loves us and he loves to spend time with us, which is what we need if our relationship with him is to flourish.

4. Time for God

A Sabbath allows us to set aside specific time that is focused on God. It is no ordinary day like the others. Yes, it is for our benefit, but not for ours alone – God is jealous for relationship with us. In our busyness we can easily squeeze God out during the activity of the working week. This commandment is given to help us avoid that.

Whenever possible let us meet together corporately, as this commandment was given to a people and has a communal dimension. A Sabbath is a specific opportunity to worship God as a community.

The danger of legalism

In the past, adopting Sabbath principles has too often been a legislative or regulatory issue, say about trading hours or Sunday opening. Or it was about good intentions. Poor Dr Johnson was full of good intentions and made a range of resolutions every year for thirty years, but he rarely managed to attend church regularly. On Good Friday in 1775 he recorded:

> When I look back on resolutions of improvement and amendments, which have year after year been made and broken, either by negligence, forgetfulness, vicious idleness, casual interruption, or morbid infirmity . . . why do I yet try to resolve again? I try because Reformation is necessary and despair is criminal. I try in humble hope of the help of God.[7]

Embracing this commandment is a spiritual issue – about recognizing the lordship of our lives, including our working lives. In short, without Sabbaths we are heading for trouble.

So how can we keep the Sabbath?

Unless we make it a priority it will never become a pattern in our lives. And ironically, we may need to work hard to make it happen, especially if our work patterns (shift or rota) include Sundays. We may need to challenge work policies or cultures that intrude into our ability to remember the Sabbath: for example, City lawyers often attend documentation meetings that go on throughout the weekend.

It may help to develop two sets of patterns, of rests and reminders, during the working week. In this way the Sabbath will become part of the rhythm of our daily life that is tuned in with Sunday – even expectant of what Sunday will bring.

A pattern of rests

God's pattern in creation was to work and reflect and then rest. The Old Testament also laid down a pattern of Sabbath years (one in seven) in order to allow the land to rest. Then there was a Sabbath of Sabbaths – the Jubilee (after fifty years) – a time of greater rest when inequalities were resolved.

In our workplace we can also develop a pattern of rests: times when we can reflect on what we have been doing and then rest. There may be such opportunities at the end of a task, on completing a project or an assignment, or after closing a deal. So rather than immediately moving on to the next thing, you pause for a short time – it may not need to take long. Paul Valler tells of how, instead of back-to-back meetings, he arranged fewer meetings and more gaps, which he used for rest, reflection and preparation. It is spiritually healthy to develop a habit of mini- or micro-rests during the day, using whatever opportunities you have – whether you are in control of your diary or not.

Brother Lawrence, author of the little Christian classic *The Practice of the Presence of God*, spent much of his life as a lay brother in the kitchen of a monastery in Burgundy. He did not enjoy his work and wasn't particularly suited to it (he was awkward and broke things), but he gradually developed an attitude to his daily life in which the presence of God became as real in work as in prayer: 'We must, during all our labour and in all else we do . . . pause for some short moment, as often indeed as we can, to worship God in the depth of our heart, to savour Him, though it be in passing, and as it were by stealth.'[8] We too need to learn stillness – even if it is only milliseconds; developing such a stillness allows us to know the presence of the Lord, the glory of the living God and his power, in whatever situation we find ourselves.

When we get a space between meetings or a break between tasks, this is a great time to turn to God. It is about developing a habit that provides us with more opportunities to savour

God and worship him, wherever we are and no matter how busy we are.

The working day can often throw up unexpected opportunities for a pause – or we can *plan* rests that can be used to bask in the presence of God. For example, a cancelled lunch may offer the chance to go out anyway and use the time to pray in a church or a park – something I often did. Or why not use taxi rides to reflect or to read Scripture from a pocket New Testament. What about coffee or tea breaks, especially if you can leave your work station for a few minutes, or waiting at the printer, water cooler or copier, even going to the loo?!

A pattern of reminders

The commandment begins with the word 'Remember . . . '
In the Deuteronomy account, after giving the Ten Commandments (chapter 5), God instructs Moses like this:

> These commandments that I give you today are to be upon
> your hearts. Impress them on your children. Talk about
> them when you sit at home and when you walk along the
> road, when you lie down and when you get up. Tie them
> as symbols on your hands and bind them on your foreheads.
> Write them on the door-frames of your houses and on
> your gates.
> (Deuteronomy 6:6–9)

Hence the Judaic practice of fixing a *mezuzah* (a small text written on a piece of parchment) to the door frame as a constant reminder. We can do something similar at work, using a reminder of God's presence without it becoming mere religious symbolism. We too need everyday practical prompts to remind us of God's ways, laws and commands, something that triggers an association. Some people wear a WWJD bracelet. Here are half a dozen suggestions that I have come across:

Computer screens offer some of the most practical opportunities, and many of us have one in front of us for much of the day. I know of some who look at the icons and see a double click into a whole new application (the kingdom of God). Others may use a discreet screensaver – a small verse of Scripture (perhaps 'In the beginning was the Word' scrolling slowly across the screen, or bold evangelists might have 'JESUS SAVES' in large letters). I am often prompted by the progress bars that pop up when the computer is taking a few moments to do something (load a web page etc.) – I ask God: 'Fill me up with your Holy Spirit.' It just takes a second (or longer, depending on the age of your computer!).

I have a Christian desk calendar which displays a proverb for each day. I don't use it every day; sometimes it is stuck for ages! But it is there as a reminder.

Some people I know use telephone rings. The second or third ring prompts them to remember that Jesus is with them in that call.

I have found doorways helpful. As I go through the opening into a meeting, I use the doorframe as a reminder that Jesus is with me. That has been so helpful when facing a difficult situation.

A window, if you have one nearby, can act as a prompt, as a kind of reflection of the face of Christ, like a mirror. Instead of gazing out, look into his face.

So often our most difficult situations occur when we are physically alone, or feeling isolated in a group, like in a hostile meeting, so it can be very useful to be reminded that we are not alone but are accompanied in our work by the King of kings.

Enjoying God

While our work has a purpose, it also has limits, and the limitations are beneficial; otherwise we may neglect God. He is described as 'a jealous God' (Exodus 20:4), in that he is possessive of the worship and service that are due to him. These limits, given to us out of love, mean that we can spend time enjoying him – in the rhythms that God has demonstrated in his own creative working. He wants us to appreciate what he has blessed us with, in a time (or times) set apart for that purpose, when we can reflect, delight and rest.

For reflection

1. How is the Sabbath expressed in your working life?
2. How might you develop a pattern of rests at work?
3. In what ways might you be able to introduce reminders of God's presence with you at work?

8. MAINTAINING RESPECT

You shall not misuse the name of the LORD your God,
for the LORD will not hold anyone guiltless
who misuses his name.
(Exodus 20:7)

Names are important. Dale Carnegie's *How to Win Friends and Influence People* which has sold 30 million copies has remembering people's names as its third principle. The book gives many examples of the power that comes from recalling a person's name.

How well known our name is in the marketplace can be important to us. We meet a new client. 'Oh, I've heard of you,' they might say, and we glow inside. Or 'So-and-so [a significant name] mentioned you.' We like it when our name gains significance. We take note when we read in the market about a notable 'name' moving from one firm to another.

We like to see our name on a guest list, in a document or report, in the press perhaps, on the firm's notepaper (I did!), as author of some publication or on a roll of honour.

Members of Lloyds the insurer are individuals known as 'Names'. Our name sums up our reputation. If our name is misused or we face a false accusation, especially in the press, we can resort to the laws of slander or libel to seek redress, so every major newspaper has an in-house lawyer vetting stories.

One of the saddest episodes in that extraordinary TV series *The Office* was at the end when David Brent, following his redundancy, tried to make it as an entertainer, based on his brief fame on TV. We witness the tragic scene when his name has already been forgotten.

When I finished studying estate management I joined an old established property firm called Healy & Baker (no longer a name themselves – they are now part of Cushman Wakefield). It was back in the 1970s and they were just ending the practice of new members being required to change their surname if it was the same as an existing partner. They wanted to avoid confusion and safeguard their partners' reputation. Can you imagine that being suggested these days?!

But a name is vulnerable; it can be brought into disrepute, even by the actions of just one person. For example, Barings, once one of the City's great names, is no more; it was mortally wounded by Nick Leeson in faraway Singapore. In Proverbs 22:1 we read: 'A good name is more desirable than great riches; to be esteemed is better than silver or gold.'

Names as brands

Names are so important that they become brands. A whole industry of patent agents and intellectual property lawyers has grown up around them. Advertising uses the power of a brand name. So much so that at one time advertisers used to pay *us* to wear their name, but now we pay them! We want to be associated with their name. Company names are important, so much so that many of the most successful names have become super-brands: the 2011 top ten super-brands are Mercedes-Benz, Rolex, the BBC, Coca-Cola, Google, Microsoft, BMW, British Airways, Apple and Jaguar.

According to a Universum Graduate Survey (of nearly 6,000 final and penultimate year students) most students want to work for big, well-known companies: 'Students associate big brand names with market success and financial strength, and believe that companies of this calibre will offer international career opportunities, challenging and varied work, inspiring colleagues and training.'[1]

As branded companies merge, they face the difficulty of holding on to the original names. I was proud to have been a partner in Hillier Parker, now part of CBRE, where the initials are too crowded even to include a reference to my old firm. A new brand has been forged.

The name above all names

The third commandment is about giving recognition and honour to the one who is the name above all names: the one who most deserves it. Some Bible translations speak of 'not taking the Lord's name in vain'. God has revealed himself to his people, even his name, and out of his great love for his people, he commands them to take his name seriously, for in Old Testament culture names were highly significant. What name could be more significant than God's own?

John Durham explains it like this:

> The third commandment is directed not towards Yahweh's protection, but towards Israel's . . . Yahweh's names and titles must be honoured, blessed, praised, celebrated, invoked, pronounced and so shared. To treat Yahweh's name with disrespect is to treat his gift lightly, to underestimate his power, to scorn his presence, and to misrepresent to the family of humankind his very nature as 'The One Who Always Is'.[2]

In Philippians 2:9 we read: 'Therefore God exalted [Jesus] to the highest place and gave him the name that is above every name.' It is therefore remarkable that this same Jesus took the initiative in revealing God's love for us by humbling himself, coming among us, living our life and dying our death on the cross. What was impossible to obey became, by his work and the indwelling life of the Holy Spirit, a deep desire within us, so that we want to obey his commands, and they become, like this one, a promise rather than a burden.

The significance of names

There are three aspects to the significance of a name:

The first is **authority**. A policeman has the power of arrest 'in the name of the law', so when in uniform he can stop the traffic, although when he's not it's best not to try! Officers in the armed services act on the authority of the Sovereign who commissioned them. Employees act in the name of their firm or the organization that employs them.

Interestingly, in Japan at the start of a business meeting the visitors' business cards are ceremonially laid out according to their position and authority.

The second is **power**. A brand name has power, as does the name of a major corporation, and many people enjoy 'positional power' due to their office (so much so that it can be painful to realize their power was not their own on retirement, redundancy or leaving the company).

The third aspect is **character**. A company's name says so much about it. Just think of the market leaders in any field. The name can be synonymous with a characteristic and is tied to its reputation.

Personal names no longer have significance in themselves, but our character can often give rise to our being given nicknames. Nicknames are common in the armed forces, where the person's surname or character, or a combination of the two, is often used to good effect.

His name as revelation

We did not find God, but it was God who revealed himself to us, through his dealings with his people – as we read in the

Bible accounts. He revealed his name to us as well. One name that sums up God's character is: 'I AM WHO I AM' (Exodus 3:14). It means God is before time, self-authenticating, unchangeable and constant. God is love. He is faithful, compassionate and holy. The Israelites so revered his name that they would not say it aloud, but if they had to they breathed it: 'YHWH' (no vowels!); and it was so holy that they would not write it. Even today the name of Yahweh is often translated as 'LORD' in Scripture.

God's name is the most significant of all names, but in making it known he chose also to reveal his identity and his vulnerability. By revealing it to mortal, frail humanity he takes a risk that it will be misused. Jesus came to make God's revelation of himself complete; in doing so, God risked us abusing his own Son. In Jesus, God himself came to us and identified with us. Jesus brings in a new era of knowing God. He is not just the transcendent YHWH, but also immanent: God with us. Jesus taught us to experience God intimately, calling him Father (*Abba* = Daddy). In reciting what we now call 'The Lord's Prayer' we have made it sound a bit religious. But it is profound:

'Our Father in heaven' – this refers to God as both intimate and transcendent; and 'Hallowed be your name' – he is revered, totally respected. These are the words of the Son of God. As such he sets the standard for us too. God is perfect and holy, and we cannot approach him on our own merits. No-one has seen God: we are too dirty. Therefore we must not think too highly of ourselves, yet we do often view ourselves more highly than we ought.

What's the problem?

This commandment tells us that God's name matters: to God himself, to us, and to everyone else, even if they don't recognize it. It matters to God, as he is holy, the name above all names. It matters to us, as by elevating ourselves we are downgrading God, which is spiritually corrosive and unhealthy. It also matters to everyone else, as our work culture demonstrates too many examples of pride, arrogance, one-upmanship, power-broking and me-first behaviour, which harms and dehumanizes people.

In Channel 4's *The New Ten Commandments* this commandment was the third to go, by popular vote. People commented: 'No point in it' or in the language of sport, 'How could we play football?!' But as Jonathan Sachs the Chief Rabbi pointed out, 'Language matters . . . it can kill.'

In our working world we have become too important – too important for our own good. And God is concerned to put boundaries round us – for our own good. We lord it over one another and we are inclined to think too highly of ourselves. At networking events we spend too much of the time talking up our own name.

God's name is seldom treated with respect. In staffrooms, mess rooms, changing rooms, offices and hospitals, in stores and on construction sites, in the marketplace and in bars after work, we hear the names of God used lightly, as swearwords or terms of abuse. 'OMG!' is now a common expletive. There is a tide of disrespect. It's not always deliberate, but rather it has become part of our culture. And consequently it is also deep in our work culture.

Misuse

There are three ways in which we misuse the names of God. First, as an **insult**. God's name is too often invoked as an exclamation or a means of swearing, rather than as a genuine calling on his name. We hear this in many offices, to a greater or lesser extent depending on the culture. The media repeat such utterances as if they bear no responsibility, and thereby legitimize the practice.

But in our politically correct, inclusive, over-tolerant age when we are über-sensitive to human rights issues, we are unlikely to hear someone swear, 'Oh, Allah' or 'Mohammed!' on TV, on the radio or in a film. So why does the God of the Christians get singled out?

The second main way in which we misuse God's name is by **trivializing** it. If we swear on oath in court or in an affidavit, knowing that not all our testimony is true, it trivializes God. We take communion at Christmas or Easter out of tradition. But the Bible explains that in taking the Lord's Supper in this way we bring judgment on ourselves. When our children were small we had them baptized, out of convention, as I was not a believer. I felt like a hypocrite for promising what I did and rightly so!

The third way we can misuse God's name is by using it to **justify**: too many wars have been started in God's name. In the film *Kingdom of Heaven* both Muslim and Christian declare: 'God wills it.' After the recent banking crisis, one senior banker came in for much criticism by asserting that he was just 'doing God's work'.

In our working lives, Christians can sometimes make things sound spiritual in a way that is unhelpful, and at worst we can close down all debate on a decision with a statement such as 'God told me.' We should avoid such over-spiritualizing, and present a case on its merits.

Consequences

Our work culture has become decayed because we have let the darkness in, through our disobedience. We are slowly but surely dying. We are drowning in the sea of our own importance, arrogance and self-centredness, rather than basking in the light. But Jesus can bring light into the darkness of our work culture and the dehumanizing grind and stress of the marketplace. Jesus, God's own Son, as he himself declares, is the way, the truth and the life (John 14:6). He is the way: he brings direction into working lives that have lost their way; he is the truth: he brings meaning into a cynical and confused marketplace; and he is the life: he brings new life where there is depression and decay. Only life in God's Son frees us to live an authentic life, to honour his name and lift him up.

We are a generation that is cynical of authority or institutions. Politicians are assumed to be lying; teachers' authority has been undermined, and their role is often reduced to classroom control; regulatory authorities are treated as obstacles to be overcome; and even the police no longer command the respect they once did. No-one automatically gets respect any more, and respect has even been withdrawn from God himself.

When I hear the name of God abused, it hurts. Because I love him and I know his character, it pains me to hear of the person who is so precious to me being abused. It's like hearing someone swear about my wife – by name. It's painful. It is a reasonable expectation that my wife should not be insulted.

When we abuse God's name it has consequences, and this commandment explains that the violator will be punished. But it has far wider consequences than that. It hurts our relationship with God primarily, and banishes his presence. We become alone and vulnerable, left to play the games that other people play, and they are usually better at them.

The workplace context

I came across a striking acknowledgment that God's name is the name above all names – in the lobby of the BBC's

Broadcasting House. Unfortunately the inscription is in Latin, but part of the translation reads:

> This temple of the arts and muses is dedicated to Almighty God by the first Governors in the year of our Lord, 1931, John Reith being Director-General. And they pray that good seed sown may bring forth good harvest; that all things foul or hostile to peace may be banished hence; and that the people inclining their ear to whatsoever things that are lovely and honest, whatsoever things are of good report, may tread the path of virtue and of wisdom.

The governors knew their place and, while we might think it old-fashioned, it showed in the corporation's early work. Below the inscription and reflecting the BBC motto is this verse from Philippians 4.8: 'Whatever is true, whatever is noble . . . think about such things.'

We should give God's name respect because of his authority, power and character:

Authority

God is supreme: there is no higher authority, and all authority comes from him. At the end of Matthew's Gospel Jesus declared: 'All authority in heaven and on earth has been given to me' (Matthew 28:18). And the authority of God's name is clearly stated in Acts 2:21: 'And everyone who calls on the name of the Lord will be saved.' In his letter to the Romans, Paul explains: 'Everyone must submit himself to the governing authorities, for there is no authority except that which God has established. The authorities that exist have been established by God' (Romans 13:1).

This helps us to submit to those in authority over us in the full knowledge that they themselves are ultimately under the highest authority. It helps us to put their position into proper perspective and thereby enables us to respond to tricky situations, such as being asked to be a party to corruption, intimidation, bullying or lawbreaking of any kind. We can resist, with the assurance that we are under the authority of the name above all names. We may lose our job but not our integrity.

I once had to face one of my superiors in one of the most upsetting moments of my working life. I had not been a Christian for very long. As an ambitious young associate, I was aware that I was up for promotion to partner in the property firm I worked for. I was called in by the very senior partner I reported to (though he had very little to do with my day-to-day work). He opened with the startling statement: 'We don't want to make enemies now, do we?!' It became apparent that he was referring to the fact that I had been open about my faith in Jesus. The conversation was heading in a very particular direction – basically that I should shut up about it. I heard what he had to say and then replied, 'I am very sorry if I have offended anybody, but I cannot but tell of what Jesus has done for me.' That was the end of the meeting; he was in authority over me and I would have to face the consequences.

My main feeling at the time was that I had let Jesus down in some way. I walked out shaking, assuming that my career had just come to a juddering halt. I headed straight up to LICC's building (only a few minutes' walk away) and I went up to the library and howled. I then met a friend there and we prayed. Later I joined our home group and cried all over again. My career progression was all over as far as I was concerned. So you can imagine my surprise when the senior partner of the firm called me into his office the next day and offered me a partnership!

It was an awful experience, but I have to say that from that day onwards I never felt constrained not to speak about my faith. Those in authority no longer had any hold over me.

Power

The second reason to respect God is because of his power: God created our world and the whole universe – all out of nothing. His power sustains it, and if he were to stop, it would all grind to a halt. God has power over all things – life, death and the whole of creation. When the humble Job was at the end of his tether, God responded to him:

> Where were you when I laid the earth's foundation?
>   Tell me, if you understand.
> Who marked off its dimensions? Surely you know!
>   Who stretched a measuring line across it?
> (Job 38:4–5)

Richard Foster tells us that: 'Power can destroy or create. The power that destroys demands ascendancy; it demands total control. It destroys relationships; it destroys trust; it destroys dialogue; it destroys integrity.'[3] And so we read about those who have founded successful companies falling out with one another as the company prospers. We see people in our own workplace vying for position and we witness the impact on their relationship.

While God's power is inherent, ours is always given. And the workplace can give individuals great power. That may be Bill McKnees in the stationery store (mentioned earlier), the secretary of a trade union or the CEO of a great corporation. But power is given, and whenever it is given we must realize that it will be taken away again at some time. So our approach to power is that we are just stewards of an office.

We can use the power we are given in the workplace for good or ill. As managers, we can choose to bless and value people, and give them what they need to do their work, or not.

I have often been struck by the plight of those who have enjoyed positional power. Some have grown so used to a working life of power due to their position that they are hurt and disoriented by retirement or redundancy. The same people that once feted them as customers or applicants now ignore them.

Character

While human beings have been given the authority to name others, God does not allow us to name him: we have no authority to do so; but most significantly we have no means of knowing him (on our own). Even if we did, how could we put such knowledge into words? One man's way of explaining this problem was to highlight the difficulty of describing one of your favourite smells, such as roasted coffee, toast, freshly baked bread, newly mown grass or fresh tomatoes. You get the point.

How are we known? What do people call us once they understand our character? I know a successful man who was so fearsome at work that his team called him 'The Beast'. Our aim as Christians is to let our character point to the name above all names, isn't it?

Responses

In giving God's name all the honour, power and praise, it dethrones 'me' – my name – which can clamour for recognition in my working life. For in raising ourselves up we have offended God, harmed our relationship with him and deprived society of the right order of things. So what are we to do in our workplaces and in this marketplace when we are faced with so much abuse and trivialization of God's name?

1. Watch our own language

Swearing is a habit: just as not swearing is a habit. If loose language and swearing have crept into my life, it will take around six or so weeks of attention to reduce it or eliminate it. But the real antidote is closeness to God. The closer we get, the less we will *want* to swear. Sometimes as in my case (and others I have come across), an encounter with God can cause us to lose our *appetite* for swearing.

It bothers God when we swear or use slang derived from blasphemy. In Old Testament times it incurred the death penalty. So let's work to eliminate it from our lives. Most of the time simply not reciprocating or taking part is enough. This can be an effective challenge in a workplace where swearing is common. In my own experience clients and colleagues just swear less when I'm around. I don't seem to need to say anything; they have clocked that I don't seem to enjoy it or join in. But it requires sensitivity, as we can easily be seen as judgmental.

2. Be prepared to credit God

We dishonour God when we fail to credit him for what he has done in our lives. If people pay us a compliment for how we got through a crisis or remained cool in a very heated situation or came up with an extraordinary insight at a meeting, then we could say, sensitively, that God gave us the means. We need to give credit where it is due.

Statements such as 'I have a faith' (or worse, 'My faith') or 'I go to church' may feel safe, but they deny the reality of the power and person of Jesus to intervene in our world – our working world. For example, I once worked with a lovely girl who I later found out was a Christian. But she never said so when we worked together. I noticed that whenever she received a compliment about her nature or for something she had done in a nice way, as far as I was aware she never gave the credit to Jesus. And in so doing I fear she robbed him of the glory.

3. Walk the talk

We all aim to walk the talk. And a very exciting walk it is too, with Jesus. But actual talk matters too – to our working community if only they could see it. In a pressured working environment there is a danger of developing compartmental-ized lives: We are one kind of person on Sunday and another on Monday. But the Bible explains that many who merely cry out 'Lord, Lord!' will not see the kingdom of heaven: 'They claim to know God, but by their actions they deny him' (Titus 1:16). A compartmentalized life also adds its own pressures, and it denies the power of God in enabling us to lead a godly life in the workplace.

The key is to maintain our integrity and to lead an integ-rated life. I recently met up with a former colleague (a non-Christian) who went on to be a senior property figure. He enjoyed positional power and he constantly had people approach him for business, sometimes with tempting incent-ives. I asked him how he managed not to fall. He explained, 'My integrity was my shield.'

4. Be prepared to challenge others

Sometimes, perhaps not very often, a well-timed and graciously delivered direct challenge is called for. And I emphasize *graciously*. The world thinks Christians are judg-mental and is looking for proof. We don't just need *The*

Simpsons to keep reminding ourselves of this – the TV cartoon family live next door to some fundamentalists who once went away for a weekend to 'learn to be more judgmental'.

How might we begin to challenge a colleague who so insults God that we find it offensive? Perhaps we might just put our hand up to indicate that it's gone too far, without saying anything. If we do think further comment is needed, we may want to consider carefully what we would say. Personally I can't think of an occasion when I thought it necessary to say anything so directly. It has never really gone that far in my workplace. Maybe as a manager I am less likely to hear it said in front of me. In an extreme case you might want to say something along the lines of: 'Jesus is very special to me. Can we leave him out of this?' Or you could respond to an insult (about a what) with a 'Who?!', meaning Jesus, which can even start an interesting conversation!

For reflection

1. How is God's name treated in your workplace? Is it an insulting or respectful culture?
2. How might you respond to repeated swearing and the abuse of God's name around you at work?
3. What technique could you adopt if you had to confront offensive behaviour?

9. WORKING IN FREEDOM

You shall not make for yourself an idol in the form
of anything in heaven above or on the earth beneath
or in the waters below. You shall not bow down to them or
worship them; for I, the LORD your God, am a jealous God,
punishing the children for the sin of the fathers
to the third and fourth generation of those who hate me,
but showing love to a thousand generations of those
who love me and keep my commandments.
(Exodus 20:4–6)

Our journey through the Ten Commandments started by looking at those that affect our relationships: coveting, lying, stealing, adultery, anger and family life. Then we turned from relationships with others to our relationship with God – what it means to retain a healthy balance to our working lives by keeping Sabbath rhythms and remembering God; how we can live with respect for God and honour his name.

This second commandment is not so much about the worship of other gods by the use of idols; rather it is about God himself and the gift of his presence to his people, who, as John Durham says, 'must worship him as he is, not as they can envision him or would like him to be'.[1]

This commandment is about who or what *really* rules our lives. It's about idolatry: any value, idea, activity or thing that is placed higher than God. Such idolatry robs us of our freedom – from guilt, addictions, fear and failure – that God in Jesus has won for us on the cross. When we put something else in God's rightful place, we become slaves again to whatever that thing is – money, sex, power, relationships, status or work.

This commandment uses the language of lovers. For if we give our heart to another, it's as if we commit adultery, so intimate is the relationship God desires with us. He made us to enjoy all the fruits of intimacy with him, the living God. And he set out the terms of this unique relationship in a covenant: that he will be our God and we will be his people. He will protect and guide us, if we trust and obey him.

There is no room for another person or thing in this covenant relationship. Idols – in whatever form – destroy that intimacy. They usurp God's proper place in our heart. They introduce 'someone else', like an adulterous lover. This commandment is therefore all about unfaithfulness.

God is highly concerned for our relationship with him. He knows our vulnerability and how our relationship with him can be displaced by other things or people. He knows our hearts and how idolatry can harm us.

But it doesn't stop there. What I do affects other people, including my children and their children – this commandment speaks of the impact of one generation on the next, and the next. If I model an addiction to work, or can't balance work and home in a healthy way, I make it more likely that my children will have a poor work–life balance, as will their children.

What I do at work affects a lot of other people, especially if I am in a position of influence. One book I found particularly helpful is *The Fish Rots from the Head*,[2] which contends that the values of top management infect the rest of the organization, for better or worse. If there is rot in an organization it often starts at the top. A climate of fear does not exist in an organization where the leaders demonstrate that they value people and are open, or where the management can be trusted.

Idols will impact on us. Psalm 115 exposes idols for what they are, concluding: 'Those who make them will be like them, and so will all who trust in them' (verse 8).

Our work culture is suffering from an unhealthy worship of success, fame, influence and money. Or all three! And it is harming us and those we deal with, infecting our whole work culture. Tony Campolo explains it like this: 'Since failure is our unforgivable sin, we are willing to ignore all forms of deviance in people if they just achieve the success symbols which we worship.' Thus, corporate life is being corroded, and as its roots are spiritual and its home is our work culture, it's not a situation which the regulators can reverse. This is why God has provided this boundary to our freedom to ensure we stay free and healthy.

Reality check

In Channel 4's *The New Ten Commandments*, this was the fourth to exit. One person commented: 'Aren't churches filled with them?!' Caprice, one of the show's participants, pointed out: 'My whole life is my image.' To bring this statement to life, the programme makers showed a member of the public actually bowing down to a full-size photograph of the model and worshipping her image. She was rightly horrified and remarked: 'If this is where we are going, we are in deep trouble.'

The cultural context

The church in the last century struggled to confront the idolatrous in our culture. Perhaps it was weakened by the First World War and the loss of faith that resulted in the subsequent growth of liberalism, or the church's failure to respond to social change? Perhaps the church is fighting against the growing dominance of self and the attractions of spiritual beliefs that reinforce self as being central? Perhaps also the church is weakened because of our exaltation of tolerance and an acceptance of so many spiritual expressions.

Fewer than one in twelve regularly attend church, yet we are a spiritual nation. The 2001 census recorded that 70% of the population of England and Wales claimed their religion was Christian; only 10% were openly atheist. But these statistics include an increasingly amorphous body of often powerfully held spiritual beliefs, many of which are shaped by perceptions of Christian tradition mixed with other influences (usually New Age). A significant proportion of the population now believe in astrology, telepathy, premonitions, psychics, mediums and faith healers.

Images of our times

What about the less obviously superstitious or 'spiritual' dimensions? We only have to examine the images in our culture, to find the dominant idolatries. Let me suggest ten great images of our times:

1. Wealth

Some of the most common images to captivate us are those offering 'the most that money can buy', whether that be houses, cars, holidays, clothes, accessories. Hence the appeal of the lottery. Usually these images are totally unrelated to hard work!

2. Power

These are more subtle. I would include images of powerful or influential people, revolutionaries, military might, certain politicians, world movers and shakers, wheeler-dealers and exclusive circles.

3. Fame

Our culture is dominated by images of celebrities, originally from the highly visual film world, and now from any form of media: music, the arts, politics, or even just because they are famous! Hence the extraordinary appeal of shows such as *X Factor* or *Pop Idol*.

4. The body

We see a multitude of images featuring beautiful people, mostly from the world of fashion. They define what we think we should look like, even though such standards are usually unattainable, leaving us feeling a failure, empty and unloved. This imagery extols the benefits of cosmetic surgery, diets, fitness, clothes and accessories.

5. Sex

The media bombard us with seductive images and nakedness. We are lured by their power to persuade us that we can be satisfied by this voyeurism; or that good sex is easy and unrelated to healthy marriage relationships. How many films portray good sex between a husband and wife?

6. Sport

Sport has a powerful role in our culture. It enables us to take part in battles, vicariously, like the Romans watching gladiators. Sport can transmit messages of successful tribes; of belonging (us and not them), winning (but not losing, which can leave us angry and empty) or overcoming. Also sport often uses spiritual language such as 'saviour'.

7. Lifestyle

Promises of a better life abound. This imagery includes property makeovers, second homes, exotic holidays and cars

– all leaving us discontented with what we already have. I once saw a Saab advert with a space beneath the image of the car saying 'Worship Here'. A passer-by had added the words: 'St Paul's, Onslow Square'!

8. Escape

In the context of a pressured or confused world, we are tempted to escape, even if only temporarily. We see images of faraway destinations, travel, simplicity, alternative lifestyles – any sort of change – with the message that there is a better reality, not just a dream: a beach, a golf course, a mountain, a cottage or a villa and so forth. We become less thankful for what we have and put our hope in something else.

9. Nature

While these images might suggest the idea of escape, they are often about the 'untouched' or about sustainability and a call to be responsible in the world. Sometimes nature is given a personal character and God is not acknowledged as Creator. Good intentions are offering an alternative spirituality.

10. Spirituality

Spirituality is usually presented as one of a number of (equally valid) options and alternatives – images of peace, meditation, mind/body/spirit zones, gurus, Eastern mystics. Representations of Christian spirituality are rare (typically showing something out of date or repressive). The TV series *The Monk* was a welcome exception.

Consequences

Notice that none of the subjects listed above are bad in themselves; but also notice that such images make few moral demands on us. The problem with these and the other images that the world offers is that, in the process of our being open to them, they have the capacity to deceive us, enslave us and ultimately destroy us.

False promise

They deceive us by promising satisfaction. They may well deliver *something* – maybe for just an instant or perhaps enough to entice us to a repeat experience. We say, 'just one more time'. But they lie about where it's leading. As we go back for more and more, they gain power over us, and ultimately we become enslaved. The fruit of this slavery looks like debt, addictions of many kinds (including workaholism, gambling, sex), poor health (mental and physical, eating disorders, liver failure), shame and guilt, broken relationships, isolation and ultimately death.

Forfeiting grace

Secondly, they rob us of what we can enjoy in God. 'Those who cling to worthless idols forfeit the grace that could be theirs' reads Jonah 2:8. When we fall for the lure of money, fame, status, things or whatever it is that we cling to, we forfeit what God has for us or has already given us. And as we yield to their power, we deny God's power; we deny the power of what he is doing in us – the outworking of these commandments in our hearts as promises.

As we become blinded by what they cannot offer, so we become blind to what God offers – forgiveness from the past (not guilt), freedom (not slavery), friendship (not isolation), and hope (not fear and uncertainty). And yet we fall for the lure of idolatry – not that civilized people like us would call it that. And we fall for it so easily. It seems extraordinary that even while this commandment was being given to Moses,

God's people were making for themselves a lifeless substitute in the form of a golden calf.

Idols in the workplace

Not long ago an Indian mobile phone operator came up with a novel way to boost business – it was dubbed 'pray as you go'. For fifty rupees you could download images and graphics of your favourite god: different keys performed actions such as garlanding the image, lighting an incense stick and ringing sacred bells.

We may be tempted to dismiss this kind of story as unrelated to our culture, as if we had no idols of our own. However, we see an increasing deference to spirits and spiritual forces in the work arena, such as feng shui and the use of crystals. Some of my clients will not use certain numbers for the addresses of their residential schemes, and developers of some tall buildings refuse to have a thirteenth floor. I know a developer who has built his home on New Age spiritual principles. One modern English city has been laid out according to ley lines.

Superstitions are common at work: in my old firm one very senior figure would not talk about a property deal unless he was touching wood. On one occasion I watched him dart around the room till he found a suitable surface to touch! Only then could he talk more openly about it. Another partner would never open a file until he had actually done the deal – to avoid bad luck. That caused a lot of loose paper sometimes!

In our offices, workplaces and institutions there is an increase in the presence of idols. In his book *Idols*,[3] Julian Hardyman explains that there are both surface idols (such as your car) and deep idols, which are the goals that lie behind the surface ones and which are what we hope the surface idols will give us. The list he gives could equally apply to the workplace – security, significance, power, approval, comfort and control. These are worth exploring individually.

Security

Work often offers security, but it can become an idol when we cease to trust God with our job. We might find that we are fearful of losing it and so become enslaved in some way. We can inadvertently place more value on it that it deserves, and in doing so we displace the hope we have in Jesus. Ultimately it is a question of trust. Who do you trust with your job?

Significance

Work offers many people the opportunity for significance, and here lies the trap. We find that we are still looking for the significance we may not have received at home from our parents or at school from a teacher, so we look for it at work. I know a talented architect who works hard. He is the son of a significant architect who never gave him the unconditional love he needed. He has worked all his life to become significant himself. But he has ended up living in the 'prison' his father built for him. It became more important than the assurance of God's love and his significance in God's sight.

Power

Even in quite modest positions we can become 'lord of our domain'. The workplace offers us power in many different ways, not just to management or union representatives. You might be a PA with the power of access to your boss, who may not even be very important. But how do you use that power? And how important is it to you?

Approval

I know a man who is in thrall to his manager. It has always been that way for him. Receiving his manager's approval is, for him, the ultimate rating of his worth. Consequently his self-esteem is highly volatile and he gets very anxious at work. Even though he is a Christian, he has replaced God with another to give him his sense of worth.

For many years I worked in a very approving environment. I then left and went to work in a smaller, more controlling environment. It was such a shock and I didn't like some of the reactions it brought out in me: when they got petty, I got petty back, in a way that I never knew was possible in me. The new work culture pushed some of my buttons, and I had to learn to respond to God rather than to my non-approving colleagues.

Comfort

For some the workplace can be a comfortable place. That may be fine, or it could be a place where a good wage is earned in exchange for little effort, allowing the enjoyment of a comfortable life. Or you might be in a job which offers real physical comforts in the working environment. Are you getting your satisfaction there? Or trying to?

Control

I have found that control – or more precisely, the need for control – is a common deep motivation for certain types of behaviours. For example, a colleague who is a poor manager but still needs to take control of everything that passes her door, in the name of good management, is actually there to meet her own need. And this need becomes an idol that has to be satisfied.

Controlling people are not usually those who develop

other people well at work; the reverse is often the case. They control others into following their wishes perhaps by being rude about employees publicly, or by using shaming language, such as 'I was disappointed . . . ' My observation is that people who work for controlling managers tend to get smaller rather than bigger, as they are not encouraged to grow.

The power to change

As the forces in our work culture are so strong, how can we change it, even in ourselves? Julian Hardyman explains:

> We will not overcome idols simply with behavioural change through resolution and willpower. Even if we get rid of one idol we will simply replace it with another . . . Instead we need to be persuaded in heart, mind and imagination that God's love is the ultimate reality of our lives. That we are loved – loved more than we could ever have hoped for, loved with a love that is passionate and jealous and committed and powerful. That God knows our sense of need for security, control, approval, affection and comfort. That he meets those needs, as he sees best, in and through Jesus Christ.[4]

In that context we can respond to what God has already done in Christ Jesus on the cross. He has taken the initiative in enabling us to accept God in his proper place in our hearts. Through the work of the Holy Spirit in his believing people, he is now working out this commandment in us as a promise, and we can cooperate with his work.

1. Surrender our hearts

If my heart is sold out to Jesus in gratitude for what he has done for me, and if I hold my work lightly as a steward, and if I fully trust God with my job, it will not have the same hold over me and I won't live in fear of losing it.

We must not give in to the inevitability of idolatry in our workplace. It is too easy to be overwhelmed, just to give in or try to run away from it all, or to hide in a holy huddle for an hour or so on Sunday in an idol-free zone (or is it?!). Some aspects of idolatry in our workplace may be too big an issue to ignore, or too serious for me as an individual to not act upon. And if we don't do something, how long will even our 'holy hour' survive?

2. Tackle the idol, not the person

The church can sometimes throw out the baby with the bathwater. Faced with the idolatry of sex, it may appear to condemn sex as something bad; or similarly with the issue of making money or acquiring things. But this misses the point. It's our motives – what is going on in our hearts – that needs tackling. Not something that is good when it is not abused. Too often Christians are labelled as being *against* things. But this world needs to know what we are *for*.

I was once asked to work on a project for a client who wanted to build a New Age temple involving a variety of idols. At first I just took on the project, much as I might any other project in the office. After all, I have a business to run and mouths to feed, I reasoned. But I became increasingly uncomfortable about it. So I phoned the client to say I wanted to resign from the project. He was intrigued as to why, and asked me round to the London pad of one of the main investors in the project, a very successful American business-man. When I met them both there one evening and explained that I was uneasy about the project, they pressed me to say why. It turned out that they were very interested in *all* religions, which was partly why they were building this temple. That opened up a long, and frankly amazing, conversation which eventually led me to telling them why I worship only Jesus.

I don't usually get the opportunity to talk to such people about Jesus, so this was another example of what God can do when I actually say something.

3. Try turning it on its head

When people refer to nature as personal or as some sort of creator force, we can reply in a way that acknowledges God as Creator. Or when people use superstitious language (luck, touching wood), we can ask them why they do that, but in a way that does not come over as judgmental. We can graciously prompt a discussion. For example, when I am asked for my star sign, I always say 'Bethlehem'. It has often started an interesting conversation!

4. Confront it graciously – in the public domain

Let us not always be silent when physical idols or images of deities are brought into our offices or institutions. We might need to speak to a senior person and suggest it would not be appropriate or helpful, or even request its removal – but with grace. Let us speak up if occult or superstition practices are introduced officially, such as feng shui (perhaps during an office move).

5. Doing away with it in our private domain

If you have ever consulted a medium or fortune-teller, or have been in contact with the occult, you need to get it dealt with. Pray with a senior person in your church. We must resolve to get rid of any object (maybe a gift or souvenir that is overtly an idol) that has come into our office or home, rather than just leave it.

But it's more likely that we are enslaved to one of the idols or images of this world: money, power or things – let's resolve now to do away with it. Dethrone it in your own life. If, for example, making money is an idol for you, give it away; if it's work, set boundaries (I mentioned mine in the last chapter); if it's power, use it for the benefit of others; if it's your looks or body, then bless others (for example, go and chat to the ugliest girl or boy at the office party).

Some imagery, particularly pornographic, burns itself into our minds, so this may require more specific help. Go and seek it. Tim Chester's book *Captivated by a Better Vision*[5] might help you.

6. Be accountable

In order to keep ourselves from idolatry we all need to be accountable, as our hearts can be deceptive. We need one another to help us check out our motives. One of the most effective ways of doing this is to pray together, to help one another see reality. I recall a time when I was thinking of taking on a new role. I asked a senior person at church to pray for me. As he laid a hand on my back as I knelt down, he said he could almost feel my burning ambition. It was a warning, but not one I heeded too well at the time, and I soon realized that I wanted this new role too much for my own good.

One of the most important things a Christian can do to stay accountable is to have a prayer partner (or triplet): someone who can understand one's working world. A home group is not always the best place. Looking back over twenty-five years of being a Christian, I would say that one of the most significant helps has been to pray regularly (and I have met monthly) with another person (or two) about the issues I face day to day.

Intimacy with God

The images and idols of this world are spiritually bankrupt. They deceive, entice and enslave; they take us back to Egypt. They take and take and take, and ultimately they can destroy. But the true and living God gives and gives and gives, and has ultimately given of himself in the person of Jesus. Instead of finding ourselves disappointed, dissatisfied, devalued and ultimately dehumanized in the work cultures in which we operate, let us enjoy the intimate relationship that God makes possible for us with him, where we become loved, valued, satisfied, fulfilled, full of hope and more human.

The one, true, living God is the great God, slow to anger and abounding in love. He deserves our whole heart.

For reflection

1. What kind of idols are apparent in your workplace?
2. Are there any idols in your own life that you want to be free of?
3. What practical, loving steps can you take in your workplace to help push back the tide?

10. STAYING FOCUSED

You shall have no other gods before me.
(Exodus 20:3)

The first commandment addresses the issue of who is first – in my life, in your life, in our working life. It means putting God first – in every sphere, including work. For the people of Israel, this gave them an expectation of absolute priority – what John Durham calls 'the essential foundation for the building of the covenant community'.[1] He explains, 'Yahweh had opened himself to a special relationship with Israel, but that relationship could develop only if Israel committed themselves to Yahweh alone.' And 'If they were to remain in his presence, they were not to have other gods.'

How can this possibly be relevant to the workplace? Or even to society in general? In Channel 4's *The New Ten Commandments*, four of God's originals were disposed of, and this one might have been expected to go the same way, but it survived – at number nineteen. People expressed this commandment mostly in terms of freedom of worship (in tune with a culture that venerates tolerance).

Context for God's people

The recital of the Ten Commandments in Exodus is prefaced by a statement. As God gave the commandments to Moses to set before the people, he said, 'I am the LORD your God, who brought you out of Egypt, out of the land of slavery' (Exodus 20:2).

This is the formulaic language of an ancient legal document. The sovereign declares who his people are and then goes on to recite their privileges and obligations. In these opening words God declares who he is: 'I am . . . '. And he gives himself three titles: the LORD, your God, and (though he doesn't actually use this term) he refers to himself as the one who brought them out of slavery – a Redeemer.

'The LORD' means the Almighty: one who is sovereign, supreme, above all others, the Creator, the great I AM. God describes himself personally as 'your God' because he chose a people and a relationship with them. He is not some abstract force; he is personal and relational. 'Redeemer' speaks of a God who *acts* and *intervenes*; he is not remote, nor does he stand aloof from his people. He has rescued them.

And the story of God's dealings with Israel in the Old Testament is one of his constant and redeeming love for, and faithfulness to, a people that so often prefer Egypt to the Promised Land – slavery to freedom. Time and again, they rejected God's ways. And he had to send patriarchs, prophets, judges, kings and finally his own Son in order to bring his people back from the messes they had got themselves into and turn them back to himself.

Patterns at work

The pattern of God's people in the Old Testament is all too often our own story. We do the same things and we take them into the workplace. Yet the God who saved his people is still active in our hearts, and can bring us out of slavery and back to himself if we let him. We often return to our old habits (how I enjoyed being significant when my name joined the list of senior personnel on the firm's notepaper!); yet we can enjoy freedom only when we go God's ways.

We have seen that in coveting we lose contentment, and that it often opens the door to breaking another of God's commandments. We see how harmful it is to give false testimony, especially to a colleague's reputation. The workplace has many opportunities for stealing, and in doing so we offend God and hurt others. We know what healthy relationships can look like in the workplace. We have explored the impact of anger and its deadly effects; how to live with our past and honour our parents; and how to respect our older colleagues. The rhythms of the Sabbath give balance to our working lives. A right use of God's name helps us to maintain respect. And by avoiding idolatry we can work in freedom. All these elements come together in the first commandment. By not allowing any other god, we remain in the presence of the one true God.

We have looked at the lure of what the world of work has to offer. Although these things are not intrinsically bad, the pursuit of security, significance, power, approval, comfort and control can become idols, if we place too high a value on them.

We have looked at money, status, reputation and all the things that can enslave us. And we have seen that the fruit of that enslavement is poorer relationships, stress and worry, guilt, fear, addictions, isolation and ultimately death.

So this commandment is to help us stay focused – on the only One who deserves to be first in our lives.

A me-first work culture

When I go to a networking event I find that I talk myself up: I describe significant projects I am involved in and impressive clients I am working for. I do all this to impress others because I work in a me-first work culture which influences me.

When I spend time with clients, they talk about the challenges to their business and the planning problems they face (the bit they want to see me about). But all too often they also tell me how brilliantly they are overcoming those challenges.

When I read the business pages I am aware of just how big some of the egos are out there. I am struck by how major investment decisions have been taken just to satisfy the inflated (and often personal) ambitions of some of those in commerce. I am sure we can all picture areas of our organization which have a strong 'me' personality in some part of them. The trouble with me-first is that you come second, or even last.

All this is in stark contrast to Jesus' own teaching which says, 'If anyone wants to be first, he must be the very last, and the servant of all' (Mark 9:35).

Saved from ourselves

Tony Campolo summarizes our condition:

> Because the world sees wealth, power and prestige as the indicators of success, we have been conditioned to seek them with all our might. But our Lord has different criteria for evaluating success. He calls us away from society's symbols of success and urges us to '[First] seek after his Kingdom and his righteousness' (Matthew 6:33).[2]

The problem

But the problem of sin is an obstacle to God rearranging our priorities. The Bible uses various images to explain sin: it is described as 'pollution' – a stain that affects our lives and those of others (James 1:27); it is a 'power' which has a real hold on us, such that resolutions cannot break it (Acts 26:18). There is a 'penalty' for our sin; it is of major consequence to God. Finally, our sin separates us from God – it creates a 'partition' (Isaiah 59:2).

This is how the problem is dealt with: Jesus came to die in our place; only Jesus the sinless one is qualified to do this.

And on the cross he took upon himself all our sin. Paul explains in his letter to the Romans:

> But now a righteousness from God, apart from the law, has been made known, to which the Law and the Prophets testify. This righteousness from God comes through faith in Jesus Christ to all who believe. There is no difference, for all have sinned and fall short of the glory of God, and are justified freely by his grace through the redemption that came by Christ Jesus. God presented him as a sacrifice of atonement, through faith in his blood.
> (Romans 3:21–25)

Again the Bible uses various imagery and language from different spheres of life to try to get over to us what Jesus has done. So in relation to the pollution of sin, the language of the temple is used. God gave Jesus as a sacrifice – that of his very life (his blood), and this removes the pollution of sin. We are purified, cleansed.

The language of the marketplace is used to explain how the power of sin is broken. The word 'redemption' means 'to buy back'; if a slave was to be freed someone had to pay the price for him.

The language of the law courts is used to explain how the penalty of sin is paid: 'justification'. We are justified by God's grace. It is a picture of a judge settling the payment, having first imposed the correct fine for the offence; or of being executed in place of the man he had to condemn.

The Bible uses the language of the home and relationships to describe how the partition of sin is destroyed: we are reconciled and our relationship with God is restored through the death of his Son.

And so Jesus effects a great exchange for us – like no other exchange we can witness in any marketplace. The one who had no sin becomes sin for us. He dies and we go free. We need God in our workplaces, and we will see him when we put him first.

The commandments were given that we may know the right ways; but the Bible says that because of sin people are unable – by their own efforts – to keep them. There is only one who can save us from the mess of our own lives and lead us into the freedom of the life God offers. Jesus came precisely because we cannot save ourselves. He came to make the commandments come alive in our hearts by his Holy Spirit, so that we are moved to act differently. But he is not just the *key* to understanding God's rescue plan – Jesus *is* God's plan to save us. He achieved this by giving his own life.

First at work?

Work is not a sealed compartment. If we don't decide who will be first there, then the rest of our life won't work either. We will find ourselves drifting back into a place of slavery. Our hearts will get corroded, and the heart of the workplace will rot unless God is central to its activities.

So who comes first? This is a call to each shop, warehouse, petrol station, hospital, factory, office and organization, to every business and to every individual. Patrick Dixon, the futurologist and Aids campaigner, challenged a group of 300 young people at my church in this way:

> If you are not prepared to put your job on the line, then you have really lost your soul. Why? Because it means your boss can do whatever he likes and you are going to jump to everything. There has to be a point where you think: 'I am no longer going to allow this process to go on in my department.

I am either out or it cleans up.' Because you know what? They have no power over you at all. The bravest weapon of the enemy is fear.

Is God first in our finances? Jesus explains, 'For where your treasure is, there your heart will be also' (Matthew 6:21). Our bank and credit card statements tell the real story of our priorities and where our hearts lie. Do we trust him with our money? Sometimes it can be much harder to trust him with our money when we have it than when we do not.

Is he first in my schedules? A glance at my diary will reveal what my priorities are and who I spend time with. How do you spend your time? Do I meet with God first in my day? I find that unless I meet him in the morning, the day is just not the same. Obviously that pattern does not suit all of us, so you may want to meet him at other times.

Responding in love

How can we ensure that the one true God has first place in our hearts in the face of the pressures and temptations of the workplace?

1. First in my heart

He has to be first in my heart. If God is not first there, then someone, or something, else will be. There is an act of will to be made every day – sometimes many times in a difficult day – in response to what Jesus has done for me.

2. First with my time

I have found that the most important thing I can do in any day is to spend time with God. I can use the time to commit the day to him and pray through the things I am anxious about, allowing him to take them from me.

However, there is a danger that this pattern can itself become a little idol. Am I just ticking a box, following a routine and serving at an altar I have made myself?

3. First with my money

I have been bad at teaching my children about money. But I did teach them about budgets and how to set aside what I called 'first fruits' – to ensure that the first outgoing in the budget is giving back to God what is his. I need to do the same.

4. First in my mind

Immediately after the Ten Commandments were given, the people of God were instructed to remember them constantly and to teach their children. They were warned that despite all that God had done for them – before their very eyes – they would still forget him. When they moved into the Promised Land and found plenty, when they had settled down, built fine houses and become well-off, and when their possessions had increased, the Bible explains:

> . . . then your heart will become proud and you will forget the LORD your God, who brought you out of Egypt . . . You may say to yourself, 'My power and the strength of my hands have produced this wealth for me.' But remember the LORD your God, for it is he who gives you the ability to produce wealth, and so confirms his covenant, which he swore to your forefathers, as it is today.
> (Deuteronomy 8:14, 17–18)

We can forget – especially when we are enjoying the plenty of the workplace. I have been acting for an old people's charity, Morden College, in London. It was founded by a grateful merchant, who thought his ships were lost, but after they came in he gave a large amount of his money, and devoted the rest of his life, to helping merchants who had been ruined in their trade. He remembered.

We remember by going back to the Bible, God's Word, to recall all that he has done for us, to get to know him and so develop a greater trust in him. Because if we do not, the pressures of the workplace will surely squeeze him out. And the marketplace too needs to remember, for what God has done is no longer imprinted on the collective memories of this generation.

5. First as one of his

God is no longer acknowledged in many workplaces. As the head of one City law firm commented to a colleague at their carol service, 'We are not here to do this, but to make money.' Yet the relentless pursuit of that goal has left us less human, less satisfied and with less meaning in our work.

What we do and how we work has consequences – and too many of us sometimes can feel torn to pieces. The Bible makes this call – and it applies to the marketplace too:

> Come, let us return to the LORD.
> He has torn us to pieces
>   but he will heal us;
> he has injured us
>   but he will bind up our wounds.
> After two days he will revive us;
>   on the third day he will restore us,
>   that we may live in his presence.
> Let us acknowledge the LORD;
>   let us press on to acknowledge him.
> As surely as the sun rises,
>   he will appear;

he will come to us like the winter rains,
   like the spring rains that water the earth.
(Hosea 6:1–3)

Let us come out – or keep out – of the closet and encourage others to do the same. We desperately need God's presence to be restored here.

6. To meet together

The most effective way of being ineffective is to be isolated. And in our workplaces many feel isolated. The more isolated believers are, the less confident they will feel about who they are in Christ and how they should behave as Christians. When we are discouraged we get fearful and are tempted not to rely on God. But together we see a bigger picture. We begin to see God's perspective

Some firms now forbid Christians to meet together on their premises. It's getting harder, but the need is getting greater. We need to meet to be encouraged, and to encourage others; to be supported and to support one another; to pray – for our colleagues, for how business is being done and for ourselves; and to worship. In central London there are opportunities to attend church meetings at lunchtime. What opportunities could you seize – or even create?

7. To take risks

When we do or say the right thing at the right time, we are exercising faith, and the God who redeems comes. We do not know what he will do, or precisely when, but he comes. So we must keep on, in faith. For he does what he always does: he redeems, heals, reconciles and liberates.

It can be risky to do or say the right thing – but if we truly trust God with what we do, we will be better able to take those risks. As John Wimber said, 'Faith is spelled R-I-S-K', because exercising faith can mean risking God won't show up. On a few occasions I have felt prompted to step out in faith at work: once to pray with someone; another time to give someone a message I felt God had for them. On one occasion I was privileged to lead a man from another firm to Christ. From time to time I have been able to minister some kind words to a colleague or subordinate. Although it was potentially 'odd' that I was doing this, the other person never felt that, and it seemed quite normal to them.

One particular time, I was with the senior partner of the firm and I was about to leave. He was the top man and a good Christian, and I was a middle-ranking partner. I felt a strong urge to pray for him and anoint him for the work ahead of him. I asked him to kneel as I laid hands on him and prayed. It didn't last long and fortunately his PA did not come in! He thanked me and was moved in some way, but he didn't seem to think it odd.

Life in Jesus

After giving the Ten Commandments, God sums up his instructions like this:

> Now what I am commanding you today is not too difficult for you or beyond your reach . . . No, the word is very near you; it is in your mouth and in your heart so that you may obey it.
>
> See, I set before you today life and prosperity, death a destruction. For I command you today to love the Lor God, to walk in his ways and to keep his commands, and laws; then you will live and increase, and the Lo God will bless you.
>
> (Deuteronomy 30:11, 14–16)

So we have a choice: life in Jesus the Son of God – or putting ourselves first and losing his presence. May you choose well, and may God bless you!

For reflection

1. How do you discern the spiritual health of your workplace?
2. How might you put God first in your own work life?

nd
your
ecrees
RD you

FURTHER READING

Ray Bakke, *A Theology as Big as the City* (Monarch, 1997).

Ray Bakke, *The Urban Christian: Effective Ministry in Today's Urban World* (IVP, 1987).

John D. Beckett, *Mastering Monday: Experiencing God's Kingdom in the Workplace* (IVP, 2006).

Eric Blakebrough (ed.), *Church for the City* (Darton, Longman & Todd, 1995).

Laurence G. Boldt, *How to Find the Work You Love* (Penguin Arkana, 1996).

Tony Campolo, *The Success Fantasy* (Kingsway, 1994).

Sir Fred Catherwood, *God's Time, God's Money* (Hodder & Stoughton, 1988).

Steve Chalke, *Managing Your Time* (Kingsway, 1998).

Tim Chester, *The Busy Christian's Guide to Busyness* (IVP, 2006).

Tim Chester, *You Can Change: God's Transforming Power for Our Sinful Behaviour and Negative Emotions* (IVP, 2008).

Ken Costa, *God at Work: Living Every Day with Purpose* (Continuum, 2007).

Patrick Dixon, *Building a Better Business: The Key to Future Marketing Management and Motivation* (Profile Books, 2005).

John I. Durham, *Exodus*, Word Biblical Commentary, vol. 3 (Word Books, 1987).

Diane Fassel, *Working Ourselves to Death: The High Cost of Workaholism and the Rewards of Recovery* (iUniverse.com, 2000).

Richard Foster, *Money, Sex and Power: The Spiritual Disciplines of Poverty, Chastity and Obedience* (Hodder & Stoughton, 1985).

Rodney Green, *90,000 Hours: Managing the World of Work* (Scripture Union, 2002).

Mark Greene, *Pocket Prayers for Work* (Church House, 2004).

Mark Greene, *Thank God It's Monday: Ministry in the Workplace* (Scripture Union, 2001).

Brian Griffiths, *Morality and the Marketplace* (Hodder & Stoughton, 1989).

Julian Hardyman, *Idols: God's Battle for Our Hearts* (IVP, 2010).

Richard Higginson, *Called to Account: Adding Value in God's World* (Eagle, 1993).

Richard Higginson, *Questions of Business Life: Exploring Workplace Issues from a Christian Perspective* (Authentic, 2002).

Neil Hood, *God's Payroll: Whose Work Is It Anyway?* (Authentic, 2003).

Neil Hood, *God's Wealth: Whose Money Is It Anyway?* (Authentic, 2004).

Neil Hood, *Whose Life Is It Anyway? A Lifeline in a Stress-Soaked World* (Authentic, 2002).

David Kellett, *Champions for God at Work* (TerraNova, 2001).

Don Latham, *Being Unmistakably Christian at Work* (TerraNova, 2000).

Alistair Mackenzie and Wayne Kirkland, *Where's God on Monday? Integrating Faith and Work Every Day of the Week* (NavPress, 2003).

Robert Mattox, *The Christian Employee* (Bridge Publishing, 1999).

Peter Michell, *Faith at Work* (New Wine Press, 1993).

Stephen Miller, *The Peculiar Life of Sundays* (Harvard University Press, 2008).

Stuart Murray, *City Vision: A Biblical View* (Daybreak, 1990).

David Oliver, *Work: Prison or Place of Destiny?* (Authentic, 2002).

David Oliver and James Thwaites, *Church That Works* (Authentic, 2001).

Rob Parsons, *The Money Secret* (Hodder & Stoughton, 2005).

John Proctor, *Urban God: Bible Readings and Comment on Living in the City* (Bible Reading Fellowship, 2002).

Leland Ryken, *Work and Leisure in Christian Perspective* (IVP, 1990).

Anne Schaef and Diane Fassel, *The Addictive Organization: Why We Overwork, Cover up, Pick up the Pieces, Please the Boss and Perpetuate Sick Organizations* (HarperCollins, 1988).

Robin Scurlock and Steve Goss, *I Love My Work: Six Studies to Help Churches Understand and Equip Christians in the Workplace* (Terra Nova, 2002).

Geoff Shattock, *Wake up to Work: Friendship and Faith in the Workplace* (Scripture Union, 1999).

Doug Sherman and William Hendricks, *Your Work Matters to God* (NavPress, 1988).

R. Paul Stevens, *The Abolition of the Laity: Vocation, Work and Ministry in a Biblical Perspective* (Paternoster, 2000).

Paul Valler, *Get a Life: Winning Choices for Working People* (IVP, 2008).

Gene Edward Veith, *God at Work: Your Christian Vocation in All of Life* (Crossway, 2002).

Norman Wirzba, *Living the Sabbath: Discovering the Rhythms of Rest and Delight* (Brazos Press, 2006).

NOTES

Introduction

1. George Herbert, *Outlandish Proverbs*, no. 642 (Everyman, 1995).
2. Tim Chester, *You Can Change: God's Transforming Power for Our Sinful Behaviour and Negative Emotions* (IVP, 2008), p. 148.
3. Anne Wilson Schaef and Diane Fassel, *The Addictive Generation: Why We Overwork, Cover up, Pick up the Pieces, Please the Boss and Perpetuate Sick Organizations* (HarperCollins, 1990), p. 67.
4. 2 July 2004.
5. *Daily Telegraph*, 7 January 2009.

1. Discovering contentment

1. John Durham, *Exodus,* Word Biblical Commentary, vol. 3 (Word Books, 1987), p. 298.
2. *The Sunday Times*, 13 March 2005.

2. Remaining honest

1. Quoted in *The Times*, Careers section, 24 March 2005.
2. Diane Fassel, *Working Ourselves to Death: The High Cost of Workaholism and the Rewards of Recovery* (iUniverse.com, 2000).
3. Chris Angus, founder of Warlock Media, in *The Times*, 1 June 2011.
4. Joep P. M. Schrijvers, *The Way of the Rat: A Survival Guide to Office Politics* (Cyan Books, 2004).
5. Iain Pears, 'A Very Victorian Meltdown', *The Times*, 9 May 2009.
6. *Financial Times*, 12 April 2005.
7. See Jonathan Aitken, *Pride and Perjury* (Continuum Press, 2003).

3. Prospering with integrity

1. Quoted in *The Times*, 24 March 2005.
2. Chris Angus, founder of Warlock Media, in *The Times*, 1 June 2011.
3. *The Times*, 18 June 2011.
4. *The Sunday Times* (archive section), 19 June 2011.
5. *The Economist*, 5 March 2005.
6. Tim Chester, *You Can Change: God's Transforming Power for Our Sinful Behaviour and Negative Emotions* (IVP, 2008), p. 20.

4. Maintaining healthy relationships

1. Andrew and Nada Kakabadse, *Intimacy: An International Survey of the Sex Lives of People at Work* (Palgrave Macmillan, 2005).
2. Richard Foster, *Money, Sex and Power: The Spiritual Disciplines of Poverty, Chastity and Obedience* (Hodder & Stoughton, 1985), pp. 7–8.
3. John Durham, *Exodus,* Word Biblical Commentary, vol. 3 (Word Books, 1987), p. 294.
4. Susan Greenhill, 'There's No Such Thing as Intelligent Adultery', *Sunday Times Magazine,* 24 April 2005.
5. Foster, *Money, Sex and Power,* p. 203.
6. Tim Chester, *You Can Change: God's Transforming Power for Our Sinful Behaviour and Negative Emotions* (IVP, 2008), p. 56.

5. Keeping the peace

1. John Durham, *Exodus,* Word Biblical Commentary, vol. 3 (Word Books, 1987), p. 296.
2. J.John, *Ten: Living the Ten Commandments in the 21st Century* (Kingsway, 2000).
3. Tim Chester, *You Can Change: God's Transforming Power for Our Sinful Behaviour and Negative Emotions* (IVP, 2008), p. 47.
4. For further information on mediation techniques visit www.cedr. co.uk or www.civilmediation.org. See also John Parmiter, 'On the Frontline: Peacemaking at Work' (*LICC Magazine,* issue 23, September 2009).

6. Living with our past

1. John Durham, *Exodus,* Word Biblical Commentary, vol. 3 (Word Books, 1987), p. 290.
2. Tony Campolo, *The Success Fantasy* (Kingsway, 1994), p. 131.
3. Philip Larkin, *Collected Poems* (Faber & Faber, 1988).
4. I wrote this verse in praise of our own home.
5. Ruth Gledhill, *The Sunday Times,* 12 April 2005.
6. Written by the author.
7. Susan Faludi, *Stiffed: The Betrayal of the American Man* (HarperCollins, 1999).

7. Keeping a balance

1. Norman Wirzba, *Living the Sabbath: Discovering the Rhythms of Rest and Delight* (Brazos Press, 2006).
2. Stephen Miller, *The Peculiar Life of Sundays* (Harvard University Press, 2008).

3. Ibid., p. 264.
4. Mark Twain, *Extracts from Adam's Diary, Translated from the Original MS.* (FQ Books, 2010).
5. Wirzba, *Living the Sabbath.*
6. Paul Valler, *Get a Life: Winning Choices for Working People* (IVP, 2008).
7. Quoted in Miller, *The Peculiar Life of Sundays.*
8. Brother Lawrence, *The Practice of the Presence of God* (Hodder & Stoughton, 1981).

8. Maintaining respect

1. See www.universumeurope.com.
2. John Durham, *Exodus,* Word Biblical Commentary, vol. 3 (Word Books, 1987), p. 288.
3. Richard Foster, *Money, Sex and Power: The Spiritual Disciplines of Poverty, Chastity and Obedience* (Hodder & Stoughton, 1985).

9. Working in freedom

1. John Durham, *Exodus,* Word Biblical Commentary, vol. 3 (Word Books, 1987), p. 286.
2. Bob Garratt, *The Fish Rots from the Head: Developing Effective Board Directors* (Profile Books, 2009).
3. Julian Hardyman, *Idols: God's Battle for Our Hearts* (IVP, 2010).
4. Ibid., p. 176.
5. Tim Chester, *Captivated by a Better Vision: Living Porn-free* (IVP, 2010).

10. Staying focused

1. John Durham, *Exodus,* Word Biblical Commentary, vol. 3 (Word Books, 1987), p. 285.
2. Tony Campolo, *The Success Fantasy* (Kingsway, 1994), p. 17.